HEARING
GOD'S
VOICE

MARK WEST

© 2024 by Mark West

Published by Passion Publications
A division of Tell The Truth Ministries International
7005 Woodbine Ave
Sacramento, California 95822
passionbookpub@gmail.com

Printed in the United States of America

Cover image and design by:
Charlyn_designs@fiverr.com

ISBN: 978-1-957101-02-6

Author contact: marklovesrani@sbcglobal.net

CONTENTS

FOREWORD

As believers, it is vital that we establish a direct relationship with God. This connection was not designed to be done from a distance. God meant for it to be a place of intimacy. Sadly, many followers of Jesus live out their walk blindly and are unaware of what the Creator desires for their lives. What's truly striking is that many don't even believe this closeness is attainable, only assigning it to those who have spotlight callings.

In this, the disconnect is not on God's behalf but on man's. We miss out on the deeper relationship that He offers by not effectively hearing when He speaks to us. This is an unintended distance. God does not want to be separated from His people. Often the resistance dwells in unbelief and misunderstanding. For those who are wavering on the possibility of God talking to you directly, know that it was the Lord's plan from the beginning. He established this in the Garden when He talked with Adam. He created man to be in continual contact with Him. It's still true today. Neither sin nor lack of realization can diminish what He longs for from all His children. The Lord is calling, and it's on us to respond.

Once understood and then agreed upon, subscribing to this is easier said than done, especially for those who are conditioned to God "speaking" in mystic/encrypted ways. The ability to hear relies on willingness and awareness. This is where this book, Hearing God's voice, is needed. What the author highlights throughout the following pages allows us readers a deep understanding of the One we are pressing to hear from. As you go through the chapters, he does a fantastic job of defining the what, the how, and the why. This brings insight to how we should posture ourselves to effectively hear the voice of the Lord. Equally important is how he identifies the diversity of how God speaks.

Not only are we supplied with biblical examples of God's speaking nature, but Mark includes ones from his own experience. These instances help translate how it looks in our current time. His transparency awards us a glimpse into what to expect from our own relationship with the Lord. Testimonies are powerful because they expose us to what God desires to do again. It may translate differently in our own lives but the core principles remain true. Mark masterfully weaves in his personal walk with God's accomplishments in Scripture to make the Lord's behavior identifiable to us.

This book will serve as a necessary tool for any believer pursuing to grow in their relationship with Jesus. Reading the Bible is beneficial but without the Holy Spirit's input, growth will be limited. This is why it is mandatory to worship in Spirit and Truth (John 4:24) - we must have the Word in conjunction with what He says to us personally. We walk away with a fuller understanding of God and who we are when this takes place. Allow this book to assist you in growing with your Heavenly Father who wants to be closer to you. Many blessings.

Derrick Kirk
Lead Pastor, LifeLine Vallejo

INTRODUCTION

I will never forget the first time I heard God's voice. I was convinced I was going to hell or at the least, I was certain that I wasn't going to heaven. I had committed what I thought was an unforgivable sin. I had broken one of the Ten Commandments! I was 7 years old, and I was in the second grade at a private Christian elementary school. The school shared the same campus as our church. The church had Wednesday night mid-week services in the main sanctuary. Our second-grade classroom was in a room located behind the main sanctuary, to the left of the stage if you were in the main sanctuary.

A friend of mine from class was also there at the mid-week service. When I saw him, we met up and went out of the sanctuary to wander the halls. We ended up heading to our classroom. The classroom was unlocked, so we went inside. We approached our teacher's desk, and my friend started opening drawers and looking through our teacher's desk. In one of the drawers, he found the candy stash she kept as a reward for students who did well in class. As he looked through her candy stash, he found a couple of candy bars, pulled them out, offered one to me, and took one for himself. I knew stealing was wrong, but for whatever reason, I took the candy bar from him and ate it quickly.

As we left the classroom and went back down the hallway to go back to the sanctuary, my mom found us in the hallway and was upset we were out wandering around in the halls. For a single moment, I thought she knew what we had been up to and about the stolen candy bars. From that night forward, I felt guilty for what I had done. I was afraid to confess or mention it to anyone. I was worried I would get in big trouble if I admitted what I did. I even thought I might have to go to jail or something.

I also started having nightmares. In my nightmares, I would dream of Jesus coming back to take people to heaven but leaving me behind. I remember being buried in a coffin and desperately yelling to be let out and taken to heaven, but no one heard or came to get me. I also dreamt my parents and sister found out what I did and turned me in to the police. Added to the nightmares, fear, and guilt was a hopeless feeling. I honestly believed since "Thou shalt not steal" was one of the Ten Commandments, it was a sin God did not forgive. I was so miserable.

All of this went on for about two years; then, in the fourth grade, God broke through to me. During our class time, we would sing worship songs. One of the songs we sang regularly was, "To God Be The Glory." The song was in a big book along with some pictures. There was one particular line in the song that stuck out to me the most:

"The vilest offender who truly believes, that moment in Jesus a pardon receives."

The accompanying picture on the page along with those words was of a robber decked out in stereotypical robber attire: black and white striped shirt, black hat, and black mask. As I looked at that picture, I knew that was me. As I sang, read, and listened to the words of this song, focusing on that one particular line, I began to feel hope and faith grow inside of me. Perhaps I, although as vile as the robber, could be forgiven too.

Over the course of several months, we sang this song regularly from the book, accompanied by the pictures. It would bring tears to my eyes because I still felt guilty, but it also continued to build hope and faith in my heart. I finally reached a point where I accepted the truth that I could be forgiven if I sincerely asked and then believed I was forgiven. I confessed my sin to God like I had done many times before, but this time it was different. I truly believed God forgave me and assured me I was forgiven for what I had done.

I am convinced God used that song, picture, and the simple phrase in that song, to speak to my heart and convince me I was forgiven. I believe He also showed me I was forgiven the very first time I asked. It would be many years later, during my teen and early adult years, when I would begin to discover I could hear God's voice on a regular and consistent basis. For me, it has become one of the hallmarks of my relationship with God. It has enabled me to know Him better and follow Him along the paths where He has led me.

In writing this book, I desire to share what I know and have learned. I will aim to combine what God says in His Word about this subject as well as what I've discovered through personal experience, which confirms what He says in His Word.

My approach in this book will be simple: I will explore the following questions about hearing God's voice:

Why does God want to speak to us?
How does God speak to us?
What kinds of things does God say when He speaks?
How do we hear His voice?

How do we know it is God speaking to us?
How should we respond to God when He speaks to us?

These are the questions I will explore in the following pages and hope you will join me in this exploration. As you discover the answers to these questions, I hope the answers will lead you into a deeper relationship with God through Jesus Christ. And if you haven't already, I hope you will embark on your own personal adventure with Him by hearing His voice and walking on the paths He will lead you on in your journey with Him.

CHAPTER ONE

Why Does God Want To Speak To Us?

"WE ARE HERE!" they cried loudly and with fear. "WE ARE HERE! WE ARE HERE! WE ARE HERE!"

This was the desperate cry of the Whos in the famous children's book *Horton Hears A Who!* The Whos were a tiny people living in their tiny town of Whoville on a speck of dust on a clover. Because they were so tiny, they could not be seen by the naked eye. Though they cried out in loud voices, they could not be heard by all except one – Horton the Elephant, who was determined to save them from extinction at great personal risk to himself. The other animals of the jungle could not see or hear the Whos and had decided Horton was making them up. They plotted together to destroy the clover with the tiny speck of dust on it and put an end to Horton's fanciful claim of people living there.

As they teetered on the edge of total destruction, Horton encouraged the Whos to holler, shout, and scream, making as much noise as they possibly could. They began to bang on kettles and pans. They blew loudly on their musical instruments in an effort to prove they were real and they were there. Finally, at the last possible moment before they would be submerged in a pot of boiling oil, the smallest of Whos let out a "Yop." At that moment the noise they were making finally broke through for the other animals to hear. All efforts to destroy them abruptly ended, and they were safe at last. They were spared because Horton, their hero and friend, had decided they were worth saving because "A person's a person no matter how small."

We Are Here…But Why? Once upon a time, God created the universe and all that is in it. In this vast universe, He positioned a planet we call Earth. The Earth, against the backdrop of the universe, is like a speck of dust on a clover. We inhabitants of Earth are like specks living on a speck.

We are small, tiny, minuscule, puny. With almost 8 billion of us here sharing this planet, there is no question: WE ARE HERE. We exist. We live and breathe. The real question is not about our existence. The real question is, WHY?

Why do we exist? Why are we here? Why did God create us? Why does He take an interest in us? What is mankind to God? Why does He pay us any mind? What is it about us that makes Him notice us and makes us important to Him?

Perhaps you have asked yourself these or similar questions. I personally have wrestled with them quite a bit myself. God is the creator and sustainer of all things. Surely to maintain and manage this vast universe must be a full-time job for Him. So how does He have any spare time to think about you and me?

God is also the supreme king over everything – the King of Kings and Lord of Lords. He is directing world affairs and human history toward a purpose He has had from all eternity. I could understand if He was concerned about a few key people – kings and queens, presidents, prime ministers, and other important leaders. Beyond these, I find it a stretch to believe God cares about us common folk too.

Personally, I feel like I am nobody special. I am not famous, wealthy, powerful, or influential. I don't boast a large following on social media. I don't have anything of great value that would benefit God. Even if I did, God already has everything He needs in infinite supply. There is nothing He needs from me, nothing I could give Him to make up for any supposed lack He has.

If I take an honest inventory of my life, I conclude I am weak, imperfect, and flawed. I often lack the wisdom to navigate life with all its choices and decisions. I also lack strength. There are times when life knocks me down and I am incapable of withstanding the onslaught of things life throws my way. I have some ups but also plenty of downs. I'm plagued by worries and cares, fears, doubts, and uncertainty. No matter how much effort I put into living well or longer, I am a mere mortal who will one day breathe my final breath and pass on from life here on this earth.

When considering all of these factors about my life, it would be easy to conclude God has no valid reason to notice me, take interest in me, or have anything at all to do with me – let alone have anything to say to me. However, the good news is He does! Look at what King David says in Psalms 8:

"You made him a little lower than the heavenly beings and crowned him with glory and honor. You made him ruler over the works of your hands; you put everything under his feet: all flocks and herds, and the beasts of the field, the birds of the air, and the fish of the sea, all that swim the paths of the seas" (Psalm 8:5-7).

God has made us special and for a special purpose! In these words, David is referring to Adam and Eve, the first two human beings. The role and purpose referred to here were what God originally assigned to them when He created and put them in the Garden of Eden. They were given the mandate to be fruitful, fill the earth, and be caretakers and rulers over all of God's creation on earth. So, because they were a special creation given a special task and purpose, they were valuable to God.

Yet, there is more. God created us for something else too. Sometime after God created Adam and Eve, He gave them a specific command about trees and fruit, forbidding them from one tree and one tree only: a tree in the middle of the garden known as the Tree of the Knowledge of Good and Evil. The serpent deceived them into taking from this tree and eating from it, and they were subsequently punished by God for their disobedience.

As time goes on from there, though, things get worse and worse. It reaches the point where, "The LORD saw how great man's wickedness on the earth had become, and that every inclination of the thoughts of his heart was only evil all the time. The LORD was grieved that he had made man on the earth, and His heart was filled with pain." (Genesis 6:5-6) From such a glorious and wonderful beginning, humans had strayed completely from the purpose for which God had created them.

So, God devised a plan. He would send an extinction-level event to deal with mankind's wickedness and evil. He would flood the earth and destroy all of mankind, thus ridding the earth He had made of all the evil man had made so prevalent. But He decided to spare someone – a man named Noah. It was said of Noah, "Noah was a righteous man, blameless among the people of his time, and he walked with God (emphasis mine)." (Genesis 6:9)

Who does God spare? It was someone who stood out among the crowd because he was not following the way of wickedness that had consumed the rest of mankind; and someone who WALKED WITH GOD.

I believe these words contain the secret to what God is and has always been looking for: God is looking for people who will WALK WITH HIM.

Throughout Scripture, we encounter others who walked with God: Abraham, who was called God's friend. Moses, who saw God and spoke with Him face to face as a man speaks with his friend. David, who was called a man after God's own heart and whose greatest longing in life was to be in God's presence. Mary, who sat at the feet of Jesus, the Son of God, and was said by Jesus himself to have chosen the "better" portion. There are many more in Scripture and history who could also be listed here. The common theme among them is they walked with God and were friends with God – they KNEW Him. This is THE reason God takes the time and makes the effort to speak to us.

GOD'S GREATEST DESIRE, AND THE REASON WE WERE CREATED, IS THAT WE MIGHT KNOW HIM AND WALK IN FRIENDSHIP WITH HIM.

This is the ONE thing. God created us to KNOW Him. He wants to speak to us so He can REVEAL WHO HE IS to us. This makes me feel special. It makes me feel significant. It gives my life and existence meaning and purpose.

What God says throughout the Scriptures fully supports this idea (see Deuteronomy 29:29; Jeremiah 31:33-34; Habakkuk 2:14; John 1:18; John 17:3; Philippians 3:7-11). In looking at these Scriptures, and others like them, it becomes evident there is a unified theme between the Old and New Testaments. God has revealed Himself and continues to reveal Himself so ALL people might know Him.

The single greatest way in which God has revealed Himself to us is through Jesus our Lord. In knowing Christ Jesus, we commit our lives to the highest pursuit and embark on the journey of a lifetime. The gospel of Jesus Christ is the invitation that affords us the opportunity to say "Yes" to this incredible offer God extends to us in His mercy and grace. Knowing Him is His heart for us from beginning to end, from Genesis to Revelation.

In light of this knowledge of God's heart and kind intention toward us, only one question then remains. Will you and I personally accept this call, this glorious invitation? Will you and I embark on this journey of knowing God? Now is the time to hear His voice calling to us, say "Yes," and begin. God stands ready to welcome, receive, and reveal Himself to us. When we say "Yes" to Him, our lives from that point on will be about knowing Him and walking with Him in friendship – forever.

My Personal Journey

For me personally, this journey began 26 years ago. I had accepted Christ as a child, been baptized, filled with the Holy Spirit, and even called by God to ministry. I went to college to study to become a foreign missionary. I had studied the Bible all of my life in some capacity, so it was safe to say I knew a lot ABOUT God. After 4 years of Bible College, I REALLY knew a lot ABOUT God! Afterward, I became a licensed minister and accepted my first ministry assignment, which was to help start a church in San Francisco and serve as one of the associate pastors.

It was not long into my time in San Francisco that I began to realize I was young and inexperienced in life. I knew a lot, or so I thought, but most of my knowledge was book knowledge. I had studied and readied myself as best as I knew how, but something still seemed to be missing or lacking from my life.

As I met and talked to people in San Francisco who were hurting, broken, and in need, it just didn't feel like enough to recite or quote Scripture to them as a means of helping them. They didn't need information or knowledge; what they needed was to know the Savior. I was starting to discover I didn't know Him very well myself and I needed to KNOW Him too, especially if I wanted to have any impact on the people I was called to serve.

During this time, I began to listen to God's voice regularly and journal about the things I heard Him speak to me. All the while, this desire to know Him, to really know Him, was growing in me.

About 5 to 6 months into my time in San Francisco, our church had a guest speaker come for the weekend and do meetings on Friday and Saturday as well as Sunday. She shared about her walk with God and how sweet it was to know Jesus as her best friend. She would relay stories of His love for her, and I could tell she was truly in love with Him. After listening to her all weekend, I became consumed with the desire to know God intimately, the way she knew Him. I took what I had received during the weekend she was there and made it my all-encompassing pursuit. If she could know God intimately, then maybe I could too. I had found the key to what I knew I was missing.

I didn't know where to start to have an intimate relationship with God. I didn't even fully understand what being intimate with God meant or what it looked like. Slowly but surely, though, God began to unfold to me what that meant. One aspect of what this meant was God would reveal Himself to me on a deeper level, and I would do the same with Him. One understanding that had become clear to me at this time was intimacy meant "into me you see." To be truly intimate with God meant I would not hide anything from Him, but I would let Him come in and fill every part of me and also deal with anything in me He found there that needed to be transformed or changed.

This last aspect was particularly frightening to me because I was sure God would find something about me (granted, He knows all of us perfectly already) He did not like and considered repulsive. If and when this happened, I believed it would become an obstacle to this pursuit of having an intimate relationship with Him. I thought once He found anything offensive in me, He would reject me. This "thing" would not allow us to go any further than we had already gone. It would become the thing that would cause us to break apart and go our own separate ways.

In addition to this internal conflict, I was struggling with aspects of the ministry, the decisions, and the direction the lead pastor was heading in with the church. He wasn't doing anything wrong. I just disagreed with a lot of what he did, especially the role he had created for me. We were at odds, and day by day there was a rift forming between us.

This finally reached a head about nine months into my time in San Francisco.

We sat down and talked. He gave me an opportunity to air out all my grievances and explain to him all I thought he was doing wrong. Once I was done saying my part, he simply said he believed the things he had set in place for the church and me were the things God had led him to establish at that time. So, in spite of my disagreement with those things, he was not going to be making changes any time soon. In fact, he informed me if I felt like I could not go in the same direction I was welcome to leave and find another ministry position somewhere else that was a better fit for me.

I was surprised and taken aback by his response to me. I truly believed God had led me and called me to San Francisco and leaving was not an option. However, I had reached a point where I was in such disagreement with the direction of the church, I felt like it was impossible for me to stay and put my whole heart into the ministry.

As I pondered all of this, I was truly discouraged and worried. I looked to God in prayer to try and find out what He wanted me to do. I needed His help desperately. If I ended up leaving, I would feel ashamed of myself like I had completely failed. Furthermore, did God have a plan "B" for me? If I messed up plan "A," would there be something else?

Amid all this worry, discouragement, and feelings of failure and fear, God spoke to me. He assured me there was no plan "B." He reminded me He had indeed called me to San Francisco, and this was where He wanted me to stay. He knew I was struggling and afraid and He met me where I was and promised to help me. He began to change my heart and some attitudes in my heart that were holding me back from fully embracing His will for my life. Rather than finding the issues of my heart offensive and repulsive and as a reason for pushing me away, He saw what was going on inside of me and the mess I was in and pulled me closer than I had ever been to Him.

This display of kindness and unconditional love truly did change me. Even though I was afraid, I was honest with God about what was going on inside of me. I let Him in to see those things and help me deal with them. They had become not just obstacles to me in terms of being in ministry, but they were obstacles that could have potentially derailed my pursuit of a deeper relationship with God. God made it clear He wasn't going to let that happen and He was more than able to handle anything He encountered in me that was a hindrance.

Most of all, God reaffirmed His desire to have an intimate relationship with me. It wasn't just my desire, but His desire also. In fact, it was His desire for me before it was my desire for Him! He wasn't about to let me go so easily.

As God began to work in me and address issues He had brought to the surface, my attitude began to change. I began to embrace my role in ministry and the direction our church was heading. I began to find joy in the things I was called to do and in serving and doing my part.

I ended up staying in San Francisco and ministering for 5 years before God led me onward from there. During my time there, it was hard and challenging. There were many more challenges I would face beyond this initial challenge, but God was faithful to help me through them all.

This was where my pursuit of knowing God truly began and where having Him as an intimate friend became my life's greatest desire and goal. All the while, I had developed the daily practice of making time to listen and hear His voice. As I faithfully listened, He was faithful to speak and reveal Himself to me, so that I no longer just knew ABOUT Him. I had finally come to a place where I could say with confidence, I KNEW Him.

God speaks to us so we can know Him. This is wonderful news! But what is it about Himself He wants us to know? Let's explore that question as we move forward in our journey from here.

CHAPTER TWO

What God Wants Us to Know
About Himself – Part I

If you could conduct an interview with God, what would you ask Him? What would you want to know? I asked my children what questions they would ask God, and here are some they came up with:

> *Do you have magic powers?*
> *What is your favorite color?*
> *Are you friends with Santa?*

I have plenty of my own questions for God as well. What is your favorite time of year? Do you prefer hot weather or cold weather? Spicy food or bland food? What makes you the happiest? What breaks your heart the most? What are you thinking about right now?

I'm sure the list of questions you and I could come up with for God is endless. Some of them might be silly or trivial; some of them might be things we have pondered long and hard about and are dying to know. Regardless of what questions we could ask Him, one thing is for certain: God wants us to know Him. He has made a tremendous effort to reveal Himself to us and make Himself known.

But what has He made known about Himself? What does He consider important enough to reveal and speak to us?

The 4 Main Things

I believe there are four main things God wants us to know about Himself. They are the things He reveals when He speaks to us.

> *He wants us to know His NAME.*
> *He wants us to know His NATURE.*
> *He wants us to know His WAYS.*
> *He wants us to know His WILL.*

Let's take a look at each of these aspects and see how God has made them known to all of us. In this chapter, we will cover the first two of these: His Name and His Nature.

Knowing His Name

When God speaks to us, He makes His name known to us. His name is more than just a word in our vocabulary. His name is more than just a title He has given Himself. His name is not an obscenity or swear word people use when they are angry. His name is rich with meaning. His name reveals to us who He is in His person. His reputation and character are associated with His name. His name also tells us who He is for us. As He speaks and we encounter Him, we discover the deep, rich meaning of His name.

Old Testament Examples

Consider the following examples from the Old Testament. In Genesis 16, Hagar had fled from Sarah after the conflict between the two of them over the fact Hagar had become pregnant with a child from Abraham. In contrast, Sarah was still barren after all the years of trying to have a child with Abraham. God found Hagar in the middle of her flight at a spring in the desert and spoke to her, telling her to go back and submit herself to Sarah again as her maidservant. From this encounter, Hagar said to God, "You are the God who SEES me." The well where this encounter took place was even renamed "Well of the Living One Who Sees Me." For Hagar, God's name meant He saw her; she was not invisible. She and her situation mattered to God, and she knew that clearly after this conversation with Him.

God also made His name known to Abraham. Abraham was about to sacrifice his son Isaac to God on an altar when an angel of the Lord called out to him and stopped him – right as he was raising the knife to kill Isaac! Without missing a beat, Abraham looked up and saw a ram caught in a thicket, and the ram became the sacrifice to God on the altar in place of Isaac. From this encounter, Abraham named the place, "The LORD will provide." God revealed to Abraham His name meant "Provider," and His provision gave Abraham exactly what he needed at just the perfect time.

One final example of God making His name known in the Old Testament is Moses. In Moses' initial encounter with God at the burning bush, Moses asked God what His name was. He wanted to know who was sending him to go and rescue the Israelites. He knew the Israelites would ask who had sent him to them. God responded by giving Moses His name – the LORD. God was telling Moses His name is "I AM WHO I AM." He told Moses going forward, this would be His name forever – from generation to generation. He also informed Moses He was the God of their ancestors –Abraham, Isaac, and Jacob. In one fell swoop, God covered the past, present, and future in telling Moses His name.

God then revealed His name through the exodus. He made it very clear to the Israelites, the Egyptians, and the surrounding nations He was strong and powerful – mighty to save, deliver, and rescue His people from those who had enslaved them; no one could stop Him or stand against Him. In doing this, He would also show the "gods" of the other nations were nothing compared to Him. He was the "I AM," and there was no other LIKE Him and no other EXCEPT Him.

Having witnessed all of this, Moses longed for more. Through the exodus, he had come to know God in a greater way. Believing God was pleased with him and considered him a friend, Moses asked God to show him His glory.

This was no small request. Moses was essentially saying to God, "I'm intrigued by what I've seen so far. You have kept your promises and worked your plan successfully with your mighty power. You've shown me some of who you are, but I want to know ALL of you. So, show me your glory."

True to who He is, God granted Moses' request! God told Moses He would make all of His goodness pass in front of Moses and proclaim His name, the LORD, in Moses' presence. God led Moses to the place where this would happen, and then He passed by Moses and declared His name:

"The LORD, the LORD, the compassionate and gracious God, slow to anger, abounding in love and faithfulness, maintaining love to thousands, and forgiving wickedness, rebellion, and sin. Yet he does not leave the guilty unpunished; He punishes the children and their children for the sin of the fathers to the third and fourth generation." (Exodus 34:6-7)

Moses' longing and pursuit for a greater revelation of the LORD resulted in this glorious encounter. God was pleased with Moses and considered him one of His friends. So, when His friend dared to ask for a fuller revelation, the LORD was only too happy to oblige him in this. He proclaimed His name to Moses, giving Moses the opportunity to know Him and discover the untold riches of His glorious name.

New Testament Examples

What about the New Testament? What instances are recorded of God making His name known? In the New Testament, Jesus' name becomes the preeminent name God reveals to all of mankind, both Jew and Gentile.

Even before He was born, emphasis was placed on the name of Jesus. His human parents were instructed to give Him the name, "Jesus," because He would save His people from their sins (Matthew 1:21). In this same passage, Matthew showed how this fulfilled the words of the prophet Isaiah, "The virgin will be with child and will give birth to a son, and they will call him Immanuel – which means, God with us" (Matthew 1:23, emphasis mine). In these last words especially, Matthew was pointing out the fact this was no ordinary child to be born to Mary and Joseph: He was going to be God in human flesh!

Later on, after He had begun His earthly ministry, Jesus made the point to tell His followers He had come to reveal the Father to mankind. This was more than just showing them what the Father was like. Jesus told them anyone who saw Him had also seen the Father! Jesus, being God the Son, was the full embodiment of God in human form. He revealed God's name to mankind in a way in which it had never been revealed before. Jesus made the invisible God visible.

Jesus also did not shy away from claiming to be God. He did this in two ways. In the first, He called God His own Father (John 5:16-18 and John 10:25-33). To the Jews, who heard Him say these things, this was blasphemy. They wanted to stone Him to death because they believed He, a mere man, was claiming to be God and making Himself equal with God. In another place, Jesus told those present "Before Abraham was born, I AM" (John 8:58-59). Having heard Him refer to Himself by God's own name, they once again wanted to stone Him to death for blasphemy. Who was He to dare make such an outstanding claim?

Yet in His time alone from the crowds, Jesus was leading His disciples to this very conclusion: He was not merely a man, a teacher, or a prophet. In the words of Peter, who spoke by revelation from the Father, "You are the Christ, the Son of the living God" (Matthew 16:16). Jesus was showing them He was more than just an ordinary man with a familiar and ordinary name. He was the Son of the Living God with a name given to Him by the Father that was supreme. He was the Christ, and as such, He would be the Savior of the world and the King of the Kingdom.

Through Him, those who believed would receive forgiveness of sins and everlasting life. The Father had given Him authority to judge all of humanity, and one day He would grant life to some and condemn all those who had done evil. He also promised His disciples if they asked the Father for anything in His name the Father would give it to them (John 16:23-24). After His death and resurrection, He would ascend to heaven and return to the Father and sit at His right hand. All authority and power in heaven and earth would belong to Him. In all these things, Jesus and His name would forevermore be supreme and preeminent.

The disciples continued with this theme of Jesus' name being preeminent. Peter said in Acts 4:12 "There is no other name under heaven given to men by which we must be saved." Peter also credited the name of Jesus for the healing of the lame man in Acts chapter 3. Peter wanted it to be clear to those who witnessed what was going on it was Jesus alone who could do these things. Peter was not looking to draw attention to himself, get a following, or receive praise from men. His goal was to be a witness to the resurrected Lord. He emphasized Jesus and His name to the crowds of people as he preached the good news to them.

The apostle Paul made one of the most remarkable statements about the name of Jesus in his letter to the Philippians. This is what Paul said about Jesus in Philippians 2:9-11:"Therefore, God exalted Him to the highest place and gave Him the name that is above every name, that at the name of Jesus every knee should bow, in heaven and on earth and under the earth, and every tongue confess that Jesus Christ is Lord, to the glory of God the Father."

The name of Jesus is the most important name any of us could ever or will ever know. God, whose greatest desire is for us to know Him, has given us the name of His Son. Anyone who calls on His name will be saved. Anyone who calls on His name will go from darkness to light, from death to life, from old to new. Anyone who calls on His name will find Him, for He will respond to the name He has given us.

When He speaks, He will make known to those who seek Him the fullness and richness of what His name means, and they will go into all the world and make His name known to others so His name and fame will be known in all the nations of the earth!

Making His Name Known To Me

God has made His name known to me throughout the years I have walked with Him. The name that has had the most impact on my life and my relationship with Him is knowing Him as my Father. As God has revealed His name, "Father," to me, I have come to know Him deeper and in several meaningful ways. I have come to know just how much He loves me. He calls me His son, and He is well pleased with me. He delights in me and enthusiastically welcomes me into His presence.

As my Father, He has also been a patient teacher to me. When necessary, He will correct me and teach me the right way to go when I have strayed. He has shown me who He is and how to walk with Him. As my Father, He has always been my strongest and best source of encouragement. He enables me to believe for the impossible, which is possible with Him. I don't have to be afraid to try, dare, risk, or act on faith.

Most of all, as my Father, He has shown me He is there always. He will never leave or abandon me. Through thick and thin, highs and lows, He has always been with me and by my side. I am so grateful He has purposed to make His name known to me and especially to reveal what it means for Him to be my Father.

Knowing His Nature

Along with His name, God wants us to know His nature. His nature is simply what He is like, the various aspects of His person and character. His nature consists of the adjectives we would use to describe Him more fully. God wants us to know what He is like, and when He speaks to us and reveals Himself to us, He makes His nature known to us.

There are many aspects of God's nature He has revealed to us through the Scriptures. Among them are the following: Holy, Glorious, Just, Righteous, True, Faithful, Merciful, Gracious, Forgiving, Compassionate, Patient, Kind, Perfect, Loving, Powerful, Wise, Eternal, Good, etc. He is life, immortal and indestructible. He is real, not fake or make-believe. He is high, exalted, and lofty, yet He is able to be close, knowable, and intimate. Let's take a look at a few examples of how God revealed His nature to people in the Scriptures.

Old Testament Examples

In Isaiah chapter 6, God revealed His holiness to Isaiah. In this passage, Isaiah had a vision of the Lord, high and exalted and seated on His throne. There were angels called seraphs present, and they were flying around the Lord and calling out, "Holy, holy, holy, is the Lord God Almighty; the whole earth is full of His glory" (verse 3).

In witnessing all of this, Isaiah became acutely aware of his own uncleanliness. He feared in that moment He was going to die. Mercifully, one of the seraphs took a coal from the altar and cleansed his lips with it, assuring him his sin was atoned for and his guilt taken away. He was then able to answer the call God placed on his life in that encounter.

King David is another person to whom God revealed His nature. God revealed His nature to David in a variety of different ways. David saw God's righteousness and justice firsthand as God judged King Saul for his disobedience and unjust treatment of David. David did not need to raise a hand against Saul as God dealt with Saul apart from David's help. David wrote of God, "He will judge the world in righteousness; he will govern the peoples with justice" (Psalm 9:8).

David also experienced God as faithful, for He protected David from Saul, Absalom, and all his enemies. There were countless times when David's life was threatened, but the Lord protected and looked after him, delivering him again and again from the hands of his enemies. No wonder David called God his rock, refuge, fortress, and shield (see Psalm 18). David knew who was faithfully looking after him and guarding his life against every danger he faced.

David also knew God's forgiveness. David sinned greatly when he had sexual relations with Bathsheba, Uriah the Hittite's wife. He even had Uriah killed in hopes of covering up this affair, as she had become pregnant. God confronted David on these sins through the prophet Nathan because David had not confessed and forsaken these sins but had tried to conceal them. Through this whole ordeal, David learned God knows everything and nothing can be hidden from Him. He also learned that God's mercy and forgiveness are great. God not only forgave all of these sins but also gave David a son, Solomon, through Bathsheba. Solomon would be the heir to the throne and the one who succeeded David as king when He died.

Most of all, David experienced God's wonderful and amazing love and favor throughout his lifetime. God took the youngest son of Jesse, a mere shepherd boy, and crowned His life with glory and honor. David was able to defeat the giant Goliath. He was able to win many great victories for Israel, and Israel's kingdom under David was at its greatest in terms of strength, size, and influence. In spite of the dangers and threats to David's life, God saved and rescued him time and again and delivered him from the hands of all of his enemies. God would not allow David's life to be cut short nor the plans He had for David's life to go unfulfilled. Most of all, God promised David an heir to his throne. God spoke these words to David:

> *"Your house and your kingdom will endure forever before me; your throne will be established forever" (II Samuel 7:16).*

This is just a snapshot of some major highlights from David's life. God graciously and generously revealed His nature to David. David KNEW the Lord, there is no doubt about it. It's no wonder David's greatest desire in life was to be in God's presence as often as He could. He delighted in God and in His presence, for he knew how good God was, having experienced His goodness so personally in his own life. Through all of his encounters and experiences with God, it's not surprising David would say, "Surely goodness and mercy will follow me all the days of my life and I will dwell in the house of the Lord forever" (Psalm 23:6).

New Testament Examples

The greatest example in the Scriptures of God making His nature known to mankind is through the person and work of Jesus. During Jesus' time on earth, He made God's nature known to mankind and showed mankind who the Father really was. There were many ideas floating around about who God was and what He was like. Jesus, by His life and ministry, set the record straight once and for all to mankind about God's character and nature. Let's look at a few examples of this.

One aspect of God's nature Jesus demonstrated throughout His life and ministry was compassion. Matthew 9:36 states, "When He saw the crowds, He had compassion on them, because they were harassed and helpless, like sheep without a shepherd." He saw humanity's condition and it moved him. It didn't just stir his emotions, though; for Jesus, compassion always led to some kind of action. So, Jesus taught the multitudes. He miraculously fed them. He healed all their sicknesses and diseases. He delivered them from demons. He loved them where they were. Most of all, He showed them who the Father was and that He was the Way to the Father.

Jesus also showed the world that God was a friend of sinners, even the worst of the worst. He regularly ate with prostitutes, tax collectors, and those who didn't measure up to the high standards of others. He accepted them, forgave them, befriended them, and showed them true and sincere love. Because He was willing to do this, He empowered these same people to leave their lives of sin and follow Him.

Jesus also displayed God's power and ultimate authority. There was no disease or sickness that was ever a match for Jesus. He healed everyone who came to Him of everything afflicting them. With great authority and power, He cast out evil spirits and commanded them to leave – and they left. In fact, they were quite eager to get away from Jesus! Jesus also displayed power over nature and creation when He calmed storms and commanded winds, waves, and fig trees. Most of all, Jesus displayed God's power over death by raising the dead. Even death itself was no match for God's power and authority. And as we would later find out, death would be no match for the Son of God Himself, who would also rise from the dead.

Jesus also showed us God's patience. All of his disciples were rough around the edges, but he was committed to them. He corrected their mistakes and showed them a more excellent way. When they were all consumed by the question of who of them was the greatest, Jesus took the opportunity to show them what greatness really meant rather than rebuke them or dismiss them as foolish and immature. When they failed in ministry, He used those times as valuable teaching moments. He never refused to answer their questions or explain His parables to them when they didn't understand. He had chosen them, and He was committed to seeing them through to God's goals for them.

Even Jesus' death and resurrection revealed valuable aspects of God's nature. It revealed His holiness. Christ wasn't just any ordinary sacrifice for sin; He was a sinless, spotless, acceptable sacrifice to God. It revealed God's righteousness and justice in judging and condemning sin and requiring the penalty of death for sin. It revealed God's grace and mercy; He didn't give us what our sins deserved but extended forgiveness to us through the blood of Jesus and entrance into a new life and covenant in Him.

Most of all, it revealed God's amazing love for all of humanity in sending His Son to save and rescue us, give us the opportunity to be reconciled to Him, and become sons and daughters. God gave the very best He had to give, holding nothing back, to redeem mankind. His generosity was put on display in the riches we are given in Christ Jesus. Rather than concealing His nature in a shroud of mystery, God wore His heart on His sleeve and showed us what He is really like through the person and work of His Son. So, it is abundantly clear from the Scriptures: when God speaks and as we hear His voice, He makes His nature known to us.

Making His Nature Known to Me

God has revealed His nature to me through the years I have walked with Him. As I have received His forgiveness throughout my life for the wrong things I have done, I have come to know this aspect of His nature. Further evidence that I have come to know this aspect of His nature is found in the ability He has given me to forgive others.

I was bullied in junior high school and mistreated by members of my church youth group. I had not done anything to them to warrant such treatment; in fact, I tried to be friends with them or avoid them if being friends just wasn't possible.

Many years later, the Lord showed me the anger, bitterness, and un-forgiveness I had held against many of these people from my past. He did this so He could lead me to forgive them. Because I had known and experienced His forgiveness for my own sins and faults, I was able to sincerely forgive and release those who had hurt and mistreated me in the past and rid my own life of the anger and un-forgiveness I had felt towards them. I discovered too, my attitude towards them also changed. Since I was no longer angry with them, I was able to feel the love God felt for them. I was able to pray for and bless them. All of this was made possible because God had made known His forgiving nature to me.

Another aspect of His nature that has affected me personally is His kindness. If the truth be told, none of us deserve His kindness, ever. He is still kind even when He does not owe it to anyone and is under no obligation to treat us with kindness. Because He has revealed His kindness to me in this way, He has enabled me to do the same for others.

Many years ago, I had a conflict with a coworker. To this day, I don't know exactly what I had done to anger him. Every time I tried to ask him why he was so angry at me, he would just yell and swear at me. This went on for about two weeks' time.

I did not respond to his anger, yelling, or swearing. I remained silent and walked away at those times. I wasn't sure what to do or say. Since he was a coworker and we had to work together, finding a resolution to this conflict was a priority for me.

As a kind gesture, I used to buy doughnuts for my coworkers on Fridays. When I went to buy them, I made sure to buy one for this particular coworker as well. When I got to work, I passed them out to my other coworkers first, saving the last one for this coworker who had been so hostile to me.

I walked over to him and presented him with the doughnut, telling him it was for him if he wanted it. He looked at me and said, "You're giving this to me, even though I've been treating you the way I have?" I assured him I was. He received the doughnut from me, and from that point on, our conflict ended. He never spoke another unkind word to me. We were friends and got along well from that point onward. Any time I approached him after that, he was always happy to see me and dealt with me nicely. Displaying God's kindness brought an end to our conflict and turned our relationship around completely.

God wants to make His nature known to us. When He speaks to us, He desires us to know Him and what He is like. His nature is life-giving and life-changing for us. His nature in us is also life-giving and life-changing for those we are in relationships and contact with on a daily basis. Seek for Him to make His nature known to you. As you and I experience Him firsthand, others will then experience Him through you and me.

In the coming chapter, we will look at the other two aspects of who God is that He wants to make known to us when He speaks to us: His Ways and His Will.

CHAPTER THREE

What God Wants Us to Know About Himself – Part II

In addition to His name and His nature, God also wants to make His ways and will known to us. His name and His nature focus on who He is. His ways and His will focus on what He does and what He wants to be done. So, without further ado, let's take a closer look at what it means to hear His voice and know His ways and will.

The Ways of the Lord

What are the "ways" of the Lord? A simple working definition is God's ways are a consistent pattern of action on His part. If you observe the things He does closely enough, consistent patterns will emerge. In similar situations, you will notice similar responses. His ways reveal the decisions He makes and the paths He takes.

It's the same idea as if you travel to another country and observe the people there. Over a while, what at first glance appears strange or random will become familiar and somewhat predictable. The unknown will become known to you. If you decided to stay long term and live there, you would not merely observe these patterns, but you would be able to adapt yourself to them and assimilate into the culture and life of the people there. It is the same with God's ways. We learn them over time and discover more of who He is, and we learn how to walk in His ways and follow in His paths. His ways ultimately become our ways.

David said of God's ways, "As for God, His way is perfect" (Psalm 18:30), and "All the ways of the LORD are loving and faithful for those who keep the demands of His covenant" (Psalm 25:10). So, what are some examples of God's ways as found in the Scriptures? What consistent patterns of action emerge as we look at His interactions with humanity?

God's Ways Revealed in Scripture

One thing that is clear from any study of God's ways in Scripture is God is a God who saves. From beginning to end, God is always acting to save and rescue people. He sent a flood to destroy the earth and man in all of his wickedness, but He saved Noah and his family. He rescued Lot and his two daughters before He destroyed Sodom and Gomorrah. He saved His people Israel and most of the known world at that time through Joseph. He equipped Joseph with great wisdom and enabled him to become second in charge to Pharaoh king of Egypt. In this role, He guided Joseph to enact plans to preserve the people through a great famine.

He sent Moses to Egypt to rescue and save Israel from their slavery and bring them out of Egypt. He performed many great signs and wonders and displayed His power and might in delivering and saving them.

Once Israel settled into the promised land, God saved them time and time again from their enemies. The entire book of Judges showed how God raised up judges to save Israel from their enemies and lead them into times of peace and rest. The stories of Israel's kings displayed God's saving power as He enabled them to have victory over their enemies. In some cases, He fought Israel's battles on their behalf and brought about victory as they stood and watched.

God also used Esther to save His people from an evil plot against them to destroy them. He saved Shadrach, Meshach, and Abednego from the fires of the fiery furnace of Nebuchadnezzar. He saved Daniel from the mouth of the lions, and on and on and on. In His greatest saving act of all, He sent His Son, Jesus, to die on the cross for our sins and rise again from the dead, victorious over sin and death; able to save all who call on His name.

Another thing clear from the Scriptures is God is a God who forgives. Though He has every right to punish sin – and in some instances, He does do just that – His heart is to forgive. He forgave both individuals and nations. He forgave Israel time and time again for their rebelliousness, wickedness, and sin. He forgave the people of Nineveh when they repented at the preaching of Jonah. He relented from sending the destruction He promised when they humbled themselves and sought Him.

There are several notable situations where He forgave individuals. One of these individuals is Peter. Jesus had told Peter he would deny knowing Him, even though Peter insisted it would never happen. Yet when Jesus was arrested and was being questioned by the authorities, Peter denied knowing Jesus when others asked if he was with Jesus and was one of Jesus' followers. He feared for his life and went into self-protection mode.

Later, after Jesus was resurrected, He restored Peter. It's interesting to note Peter denied Jesus 3 times, and Jesus asked Peter 3 times if he loved Him. For each instance of failure, Jesus gave Peter the same number of opportunities to make things right. Peter would later become a bold and fearless preacher of the good news once the power of the Holy Spirit came upon him. This would not have been possible if he had not received forgiveness for his earlier failure.

Another noteworthy individual whom God forgave was the Apostle Paul. Here was a person who executed Christians and convinced himself he was right and justified in doing so. He was certain he was defending God's honor and being zealous for God and his law. Then one day, on his way to Damascus to continue his mission of persecution, he was confronted by the resurrected Jesus. Jesus revealed to him he had been opposing God, not serving God or His purposes. Paul, as a result of this encounter, became a follower of Jesus and was given his commission from God to be an apostle and preach the gospel to Jews and Gentiles. He became the famous apostle to the Gentiles, taking the good news everywhere throughout the Gentile world.

In his letters to the churches, it is evident to him, God had shown him great kindness and mercy for having forgiven him for his earlier mistakes. God gave him the opportunity to proclaim the good news of Jesus he had initially opposed. Paul knew it was by God's grace and forgiveness he was saved and afforded a new lease on life. Having been forgiven, he made it his mission to give everything he had to serve

Christ Jesus, even when he faced persecution, and it would eventually lead to his own death as a martyr.

Another of God's ways that is clear in the Scriptures is God rewards faith. Those who believe and put their trust in Him are the ones who saw Him move on their behalf. Let's look at some examples of this.

The very first example in Scripture of God rewarding faith is Abel. Abel was one of Adam and Eve's sons. From the Scriptures, we learn he offered to God better sacrifices than his brother Cain. In Genesis chapter 4 it states "Abel brought fat portions from some of the firstborn of his flock" (Genesis 4:4a). God's response to Abel's offering was "He looked with favor on Abel and his offering" (Genesis 4:4b).

Abel brought God the choicest and best he had, the "fat portions from the firstborn of his flock." God's response to this was to bless Abel with plenty and abundance. Abel had learned when you give God the best you have to offer God in turn blesses you and all you have. His brother, Cain, didn't offer God the best he had and was not blessed by God in the same way his brother was. Faith was the difference between the two brothers. Abel believed God deserved his very best, and in giving God his very best, he was rewarded and commended by God and was later listed as one of the great heroes of faith (see Hebrews 11).

Another great example of God rewarding faith is the prophet Elijah . When we first encounter Elijah in I Kings chapter 17, he had made a bold declaration of faith to King Ahab that there would be no dew or rain in the land except if he said so! At the beginning of the very next chapter, we find out it had been 3 years since Elijah declared this, and since that time, there had been no rain in the land! It had to take faith to make such a powerful declaration, and God rewarded it by making Elijah's words come true.

Then, at the beginning of chapter 18, God spoke to him that now would be the time for there to be rain upon the land again. After his showdown with the prophets of Baal, in which God sent fire from heaven to consume the sacrifice Elijah had set up to show the Israelites once and for all who the true God was, Elijah declared to King Ahab, "Go eat and drink, for there is the sound of heavy rain" (I Kings 18:41).

After Ahab departed, Elijah went with his servant to the top of Mount Carmel and bent down to the ground with his face between his knees. While he did this, he told his servant to go check for rain. The servant saw nothing the first six times, but on the seventh time he checked, the servant reported to him that he saw a cloud the size of a man's hand rising from the sea. Elijah's faith that there would be rain as God had said meant he would not give up until the sky produced a sign rain was coming. God rewarded this faith by sending forth the rain He had promised Elijah.

One final example of God rewarding faith is the Roman centurion who came to Jesus. He asked Jesus to heal his critically ill servant. He demonstrated his faith in Jesus by coming and asking him to heal his servant. He took his faith one step further by telling Jesus he didn't even need to come to his home to heal the servant. He knew Jesus to be a man of great authority like himself, and he believed if Jesus merely gave the order, it would be done.

The Roman centurion understood authority because when he gave orders to others, he knew they would be carried out. He took that understanding and applied it in faith to his conversation with Jesus. He knew if Jesus said the servant would be well, he indeed would be well. Jesus not only rewarded the centurion's faith by healing the servant but also made a point to commend the man's faith to the crowd following Him. He told the crowd the centurion's faith was greater than anyone else in Israel! Having encountered the man's great faith, Jesus was amazed and pleased. He gladly rewarded his faith in healing the servant, who was healed at that very moment.

God's Ways in My Life

In my own life, I have seen God demonstrate His ways. Over the years of walking with Him, I have seen Him save me, forgive me, reward my faith, direct my paths, answer my prayers, provide for my needs, keep His promises, and on and on. I have observed His consistent patterns of action over and over again and can say because of this, I have come to know His ways. Let me offer a personal example of this.

Three years ago, the owner of the company I worked for announced he was retiring and selling the business to a new owner. The new owners were going to be his brother and his sister-in-law. Somewhere along this process of transition, his brother and sister-in-law decided to back out of the deal and not buy the company after all.

I presented to him the idea of waiting to see if I and my fellow employees wanted to buy the company together and take over the business. So, he allowed us to think about it and discuss it amongst ourselves. However, he let us know if we chose not to do so, he was going to close the business down at the end of the year and fully retire.

After praying about it, the Lord told me I was not to be part of buying and owning the business. He told me He was going to put me in a better, upgraded position than I was in now. He told me He was going to pour out favor in abundance and improve my circumstances, so I was better off than before. He also told me to wait and at the right time, He would reveal to me what He had for me.

In all the years I had been on my own, I had never been unemployed. Also, every job I ever had was perfectly suited to my needs at that time in my life. Having seen God demonstrate this over and over again, I was confident whatever He had in store for me was good and worth waiting for.

For three days, I asked the Lord to reveal His plans, and for three days He told me He wasn't going to talk to me about it that day and to keep waiting. After these three days, the last of my coworkers had made up their minds not to buy the business. On the very next day, the Lord announced today was the day He would show me what He had for me.

Later that morning, I got a call from a friend of mine in the business who told me she had spoken to the managers of a company similar to mine just down the road from where I was working. She had told them about me and gave them a glowing review of who I was and what I could bring to their company. This sparked their interest in sitting down to talk to me and interview me!

I had not really even begun to look for what God had for me and here was an opportunity being dropped into my lap! I set up an interview with them, and I knew in that interview based on everything they presented to me it was exactly what God had spoken about and told me He had readied and prepared in advance for me. In the time I have been with this new company, I can confirm it is everything He told me and promised me and so much more. Through this transition, God provided for my needs, rewarded my faith, answered my prayers, directed my path, and kept His promises. In doing all of this, He once again showed me His ways in a way only He could do.

The Will of God

Along with His name, His nature, and His ways, God also wants to make known His will to us. So first, let me ask the obvious question: What is the will of God?

God's will is His design for all things, the way He created things to be. His will for us is to experience life the way He designed it for us. God's will for us also includes His standards for living and being. Some people call this His moral will. His moral will is summed up in the two great commandments – to love God and to love our neighbor as ourselves. Most important of all, God's will include His plan and purpose for the ages and His work through Jesus and the Holy Spirit to accomplish His plan and purpose. His great mission is to save us all from our sin and from death, to reconcile us to Himself, to make us sons and daughters who will know Him, love and be loved by Him, rule, and reign with Him, and be with Him forever.

God's will can be broken down further into two simple categories: His general will and specific will. His general will is His will as it applies to ALL people without exception. So, for example, God wants us to obey Him, trust Him, love Him, love others, pray, worship, live by His moral standards, etc. All of these things could be categorized as His general will since these things apply to everyone.

I believe God also has a specific will for each and every one of us. We each have a unique assignment from God, and this is His specific will for us. We are not all called to do the same thing; God has a plan for each of us and a role for us to play. So, for example, Paul was called by God to be an apostle to the Gentiles. This was God's specific will for Paul. It was his unique assignment from God.

But Paul also knew what was true for him was also true for all of his fellow believers. To that end, Paul instructed believers about the gifts of God given to the body of Christ. These gifts consisted of roles, functions, and abilities God has given to individual believers so they can serve Him and their fellow believers. In discovering what those gifts are and in operating in those gifts, believers would be identifying God's specific will for their lives and contributing their unique part to the greater whole. The Holy Spirit is the source of these different kinds of gifts (see I Corinthians 12:4), so as believers looked to Him, He would make known what gifts He had for them and how to use them properly to serve the church and the world.

God's Will Revealed in Scripture

The Scriptures contain numerous examples of God speaking and making known His will. Let's look at two examples of this – one from the Old Testament and one from the New Testament.

In the Old Testament, one of the most significant instances in which God revealed His will was in giving the law to His people through Moses. God wanted His people to know how He wanted them to live. He wanted them to know how to worship Him, love Him, honor Him, and obey Him. He also wanted them to know how to treat one another and to love one another. He wanted His people to be holy – set apart for Him. He did not want them to live and behave like the other nations. They were His special people, and He wanted their lives to demonstrate that. His law covered every aspect of their lives, so in any and every situation that would arise, they would know what His will was and how to respond and act. He did not keep them in the dark but made His will known to them so they could walk with Him in the light and be a light to the other nations that did not know Him.

One excellent example of God revealing His will in the New Testament is found in Acts 13. The church in Antioch was meeting together, praising God, and praying and fasting. While they were doing this, the Holy Spirit spoke to them about Barnabas and Saul. He had an assignment for them to carry out, and He spoke to the believers there to send them off to do the work He had for them to do. This would result in Barnabas and Saul going into the Gentile lands on their first missionary journey where they proclaimed the good news to both Jews and Gentiles.

Many lives would be powerfully touched by their work, and they would see the first fruits of Gentile converts from this first endeavor. Saul (who would later go by Paul) would continue to venture out into Gentile lands throughout the course of his life and ministry. He knew by revelation this was God's specific will for his life and his unique assignment from Him. He gave his all to fulfill and complete the work he was given to do.

God's Will in My Life

Let me share an example of God revealing His will in my own life. Many years ago, when I was a teenager, I believe God called me to go into ministry. So as a step in that direction, I went to a Christian college to study the Bible and ministry to prepare myself for this calling. At the beginning of my senior year, I started to consider the possibility of going to graduate school, and so I began to look at options for graduate school so I could pursue getting a master's degree after I finished my bachelor's degree.

The graduate school I was most interested in attending was only an hour away from the college I was attending. I found out they were having a campus day for prospective new students, so I signed up to go and check it out. While I was there, I had this feeling inside of me that something wasn't right. I left that day knowing at the very least I didn't want to go to graduate school there, so maybe that meant I should keep searching until I found a graduate school that was the right fit for me.

Meanwhile, I applied for and got an on-campus position as a resident assistant. The compensation for this position would cover my room and board as well as pay me a small salary every month. When I looked at the costs for my senior year and my financial needs with this new position and its benefits factored in, I discovered two things. First of all, I wasn't going to need to take out a loan for that year. Second, I wasn't going to need to work an off-campus job anymore, so I quit my off-campus job.

Not only did I leave the off-campus job I had been at since my freshman year, but I also stopped attending the church I had been going to since my freshman year. I had thought perhaps there would be an opportunity to be mentored there and maybe a position might open up for me to be a staff member there, but that had not materialized. So, for that and some other reasons, I decided instead to attend the church across the campus from the college.

The more graduate schools I began to look at, the more I began to get the feeling I wasn't meant to go to graduate school – at least not right after graduating with my bachelor's degree. Also, with no job beyond the school year, no church I was committed to, and school about to be done, I began to sense my desire to stay in the area was not in God's plans for me. I viewed everything happening as though the tent stakes I had put down, were being pulled up. God had somewhere else He wanted me to go and something else He wanted me to do; but what was it? I honestly had no clue at that point.

I took all of this to God in prayer. At this point, all of my own plans and own understanding had left me with nothing. I asked God to show me where He wanted me to go and what my next step in life should be. With Christmas break nearing, I asked God to give me an answer over my Christmas break.

The first weekend home from school for Christmas break, my family (mom, dad, and sister) and I got together with some friends who were missionaries. These same friends had been on staff at the church I grew up in. They had served for the last four years as missionaries in Africa. They were back on furlough at that time. We got together to go see the Nutcracker and go to dinner.

While we were at dinner, a conversation came up about my plans after college. I let them know I wasn't sure what I was going to be doing yet but was praying about my next step. They were kind of in the same boat, as they were praying about whether they were supposed to return to Africa or take a different direction at God's leading.

A few days after our time together, they phoned me at my parents' house. They disclosed to me they were leaning towards staying in the US and starting a church in San Francisco. They had been praying since our time together about whom they should invite to join them to help start the church, and they felt strongly they were supposed to invite me to join the team they were forming. They asked me to pray about it and get back to them with an answer.

I admit at that moment, I wanted to tell them yes. I was sure God was giving me the answer to my prayers, and this was the direction He wanted me to take in His will for my life. Still, I prayed about it and waited. I wanted to see if any other opportunities might come my way before my Christmas break was over.

At the end of my Christmas break, no other direction or opportunities had emerged. By this, I knew God's leading for me was to join their team to start a church in San Francisco. God also reminded me of something I had prayed for a couple of years back. I had asked Him to show me here at home how to be a missionary, and here was an opportunity to be a missionary at home in the US!

So, God spoke to me in a way I heard His voice, and His will became clear to me. After graduation, I headed straight to San Francisco. I ended up staying there a little over 5 years and helped start a church there.

My experience there was life-changing in so many ways. It was there I began to hear God's voice regularly and consistently. It was also there I truly began to know God and where He would reveal to me this was the great purpose for which He created me and all of mankind. This truth would change my life and ministry permanently going forward. It has formed the core of why I seek Him and desire to hear His voice and why I am writing this book. He wants to be known and has made ways for us to know Him – to know His name, His nature, His ways, and His will.

As we move on from here, we are going to explore how God speaks and makes Himself known to us. The ways He speaks form the pathways that lead us to Him. Let's now take a closer look at how He speaks to us and the ways He employs to communicate with us.

CHAPTER FOUR

How Does God Speak To Us? – Part I

I have always been fascinated and impressed by ventriloquists. Ventriloquists have developed the skill of speaking without moving their mouths or faces. Many ventriloquists are comedians. They have a puppet they bring out on stage with them and have a conversation with them as though they are a real person and not a puppet. They typically create a unique and funny voice for the puppet different from their own. The interaction between the comedian and puppet is fun to watch and often quite hilarious.

In watching ventriloquists as a kid, I was always curious to know how they did it. Was it some kind of magic trick? What was the secret to how they could speak like that? How long did it take to learn how to do that? Was it hard to learn? If I found a book on ventriloquism, could I learn how to develop and possess this skill too?

Maybe you feel the same way about how God speaks. You believe He does speak, but how He speaks seems to be shrouded in mystery. Is He also like a ventriloquist? Does He just find some random person and start moving their mouths and speaking His words through them? Or does He speak in some other way or ways?

I can remember early on in my life struggling with hearing God's voice because I didn't quite know or understand how He spoke in the first place. Fortunately, God has not kept how He speaks a mystery from us. He has not made hearing His voice accessible only to a select few. He has revealed through His Word how He speaks, and so it is something we can all learn and know.

How Does God Speak to Us?

So, what is God's secret? How does He do it? And when He does speak to us, is it in a cookie-cutter, one-size-fits-all kind of way? Or does God employ a multitude of ways to try and communicate with us?

Any study of the Scriptures and of nature shows God is a creative God. He created all of the varieties of plants, animals, insects, etc. He created great variety in mankind. Thanks to the discovery and study of DNA, we have learned each one of us is unique. We are one of a kind, even though there are billions of us. Even something as simple as a snowflake is unique; no two are exactly alike. God possesses the ability to create and do so with variety so everything He creates is unique and special.

So, what does that have to do with how God speaks to us? Well, I believe God also possesses the ability to speak to us in a variety of different ways and does just that. While the Scriptures show there are some primary ways God uses to speak to us and some ways are more common than others, I still believe God can and does speak to us in a variety of ways.

Furthermore, I believe when He speaks to us individually, He communicates to each of us in a very personalized way. He knows each of us intimately, so He knows how to communicate with us in a way that will get His message through to us.

Scripture records a time when God spoke to a man through a donkey! Scripture also records a time when God made a human hand appear and write a message on a wall! God is not beyond employing creative and unusual means to communicate with us. These examples are more one-time exceptions and not the rule. That said, let's start by looking at the primary ways God speaks to us.

I believe today, God uses two primary ways to speak to us: His Words in the Scriptures and the Holy Spirit of God. Let's first take a look at the Scriptures.

The Holy Scriptures

So, what exactly are the Scriptures? What purpose are they meant to serve? Why has so much effort been made to preserve the Scriptures for thousands of years down to the present day? Why has there been so much care and effort put into translating the Scriptures into other languages beyond the original languages? Also, why have there been attempts to ban, burn, and destroy the Scriptures throughout history? What is it about the Scriptures that make them so important and special?

The Scriptures – the sixty-six books from Genesis to Revelation – are more than just a mere book. They contain the Words of God, the story of God's dealings with mankind, and together they form a special revelation of God to mankind. The Scriptures contain the things revealed that belong to us and the generations before and after us. They reveal to us who God is in His nature, character, and ways. They reveal to us who we are to God, how He made us, and why He made us. They reveal His will and plans for us. They reveal His heart for us. Ultimately, they reveal Jesus to us and are meant to lead us and point us to Him. Through the Scriptures, God has given us sufficient knowledge of Himself so we can know and follow Him. Let me elaborate on a few of these key ideas.

In II Timothy 3:15, Paul reminds Timothy how "From infancy, you have known the Holy Scriptures, which are able to make you wise for salvation through faith in Christ Jesus." Paul acknowledges here the great worth of the Scriptures to Timothy and all mankind. Through them, we receive the wisdom from God that leads us to salvation through Jesus.

Jesus himself affirmed this in a conversation with the Jews who opposed Him and His ministry. In John 5:39-40, Jesus says these words: "You diligently study the Scriptures because you think that by them you possess eternal life. These are the Scriptures that testify about ME, yet you refuse to come to me to have life."

From these two passages, we see God's purpose revealed in giving us the Scriptures. The Scriptures are meant to point us to Jesus. They serve as both a signpost and a road map for us. They are meant to lead us to God through Jesus. They are meant to give us knowledge of salvation and of the Savior. They point the way to the One who called Himself the Way. Through them, God speaks to those who will listen and heed His words. In doing so, we find salvation and life. We find Him. The Scriptures are a means to an end because they point us to the ultimate destination. They are not the destination themselves, which was the mistake the Jews had made that Jesus was trying so hard to correct. They had the

Scriptures but missed the point of the Scriptures; or better yet, they missed WHO the Scriptures were trying to point them to, meaning Jesus.

The Scriptures also contain valuable instructions for how to live life here in our time on earth. Someone came up with the acronym for the word "BIBLE" – Basic Instructions Before Leaving Earth. This is actually a helpful description of one of the main purposes God had for giving us the Scriptures. The Scriptures definitely should be viewed as an instruction manual for life. This idea is supported in II Timothy 3:16-17, where Paul declared to Timothy, "All Scripture is God-breathed and is useful for teaching, rebuking, correcting and training in righteousness, so that the man of God may be thoroughly equipped for every good work." (emphasis mine)

This verse highlights the different uses for the Scriptures – teaching, correcting, rebuking, and training. These summarize the main reasons that God gave the Scriptures to us. Through them we are taught by God – to know Him, to know His name, nature, ways, and will. Through them we are taught how to navigate this life on earth and are given wisdom for living. The Scriptures contain instructions for how to conduct ourselves in various roles and relationships. The Scriptures are very down-to-earth and practical, containing advice on marriage, raising children, managing money, handling conflict, etc.

The Scriptures are also given to us to guide and help us stay on God's course. They set the standard for our lives so if we compare where we are to where the Scriptures indicate we should be, we can course-correct. Sometimes the Scriptures can be harsh, and at times they contain a solid rebuke for us. When they do, they remind us not to harden our hearts but to heed the correction, rebukes, and warnings being given for our good.

Finally, the Scriptures will repeat themselves. This repetition is vital for our training. Someone pointed out the command "Do not fear" is mentioned 365 times in the Scriptures so once a day for an entire year we can be reminded not to fear. God says things over and over again, so those things become ingrained in us. This is God's ultimate goal for His Word: that it would live in our hearts and form the fabric of who we are and all we do as we live out our lives on earth. If we allow His word to speak to us in these various ways, we will become equipped for every good work and ready for whatever comes our way each day.

Finally, I am convinced God intended the Scriptures to be a love letter from His heart to us. The most often quoted verse from the Scriptures is John 3:16. This Scripture tells us God loves us and He sent His Son, Jesus, for us, and by believing in Jesus, we will have eternal life.

The Apostle Paul tells us God is for us and not against us. The proof of this is His sending of His Son Jesus. Jesus carried out God's eternal plan to become the sacrifice for sin for all of humanity and the way to receive forgiveness, peace with God, and reconciliation with God. On this last thing, Paul says while we were yet sinners and enemies of God, Christ died to become the way for us to be reconciled to God.

God takes the initiative in love by loving us first and foremost. He did not wait for us to figure things out, to realize we were far from Him, to recognize He was missing from our lives, and we needed Him. Rather, He saw our need and was moved by His heart of love to meet our greatest need, which is Him, our Savior from sin and death. In Jesus, we see God coming to us, not waiting for us to come to Him. We see, through Jesus, God seeking us out and finding us. We see the greatest love ever put on display in all that Jesus said and did and through His supreme act of laying down His life for us.

Why does He do all of this? So, we can become the children of God! The Apostle John stated it this way, "How great is the love the Father has lavished on us, that we should be called children of God! And that is what we are!" (I John 3:1). Through the Scriptures, we learn God's plan includes us being adopted into His family and becoming His sons and daughters forever! Furthermore, we are not just adopted into any old family, but into God's royal family! Whatever we were before we came to Him, we are now made royal children of God when we accept Christ and receive forgiveness and reconciliation.

And as children, we get to receive and revel in God's great love for us! We get to know how wide, long, high, and deep His love for us is. We get to spend all of eternity knowing and receiving His unequaled love for us. The Scriptures record all of this good news for us in the hope we will believe and come to Him. It is His heart to bring us near, embrace us, and make us His own forever. Thus, the Scriptures are like a love letter revealing His heart of unending, undying love for us.

The Holy Spirit

Along with the Scriptures, the other primary way God speaks to us is by the Holy Spirit. The two go hand in hand and form the perfect complement to one another. If the Scriptures are the book, the Holy Spirit is the one who inspired the authors. If the Scriptures are the road map, the Holy Spirit is the guide who made the map and knows full well how to help us understand where we are going and lead us there. If the Scriptures are the instruction manual, then the Holy Spirit is the all-wise professor who can interpret what it says and teach and give us understanding. If the Scriptures show what God wants us to do, the Holy Spirit is the one who empowers us to do it. Finally, if the Scriptures are the love letter, then the Holy Spirit is the one who enables us to know and experience the love about which they speak to us.

The Scriptures themselves confirm these things about the Holy Spirit. For example, the Apostle Peter says this about the Scriptures and the Holy Spirit: "Above all, you must understand that no prophecy of Scripture came about by the prophet's own interpretation. For prophecy never had its origin in the will of man, but men spoke from God as they were carried along by the Holy Spirit" (2 Peter 1:20-21, emphasis mine). Peter is saying here the prophets of old spoke as the Spirit moved them, enabling them to deliver the messages He inspired. The two indeed go hand in hand. We have the Scriptures, which came from God through men; and we have the Holy Spirit, who had a role in creating what we now have as Scripture.

Jesus also spoke at length about the coming of the Holy Spirit and His role in the lives of the disciples and all future believers. He referred to the Holy Spirit as the One who would teach, instruct, and give them understanding. As recorded in John chapter 14, Jesus promised to ask the Father to send the Holy Spirit to His followers to be with them forever. Jesus told them the Holy Spirit would live with them and be in them. When Jesus left them, the Holy Spirit would take His place in their lives so they would not be abandoned orphans. It is the Holy Spirit, according to Jesus, who would teach them all things and remind them of everything He had said to them. Since Jesus' time with them was short, the Holy

Spirit would come to continue His work and pick up where He left off with the disciples.

In another place, as recorded in John chapter 16, Jesus told His disciples more about the Holy Spirit's coming and His role in their lives. Jesus told them when the Holy Spirit comes; He will guide them into all truth. He will speak to them and tell them about things that pertain to the future. He will bring glory to Jesus by taking from what belongs to Jesus and making it known to them. So, we can see from Jesus' words to His disciples they were to expect the Holy Spirit to speak to them, teach them, guide them, and reveal things to them. His presence and work were not just intended to be only for them but for all believers and followers of Jesus since He was coming to stay with us forever.

Finally, the Holy Spirit was given to us to have an empowering role in our lives. He was sent to give us the power to witness to others the good news about Jesus (Acts 1:8). He also works in the lives of non-believers to bring them to the place where they ask, "What must I do to be saved?" (Acts 2:37 & Acts 16:30). He not only teaches us and leads us into what is right but also enables us to do what is right (Romans 8:1-17). In addition to this, He makes God's great and amazing love known to us and enables us to know and experience that love (Romans 5:5). In all of these things, the Holy Spirit's power is essential to bringing about everything God wants to be accomplished in the earth.

The Holy Spirit in Action

The book of Acts paints us an invaluable picture of the Holy Spirit alive and active in the lives of the disciples and the early church. Let's take a look at some examples that show

Him speaking to them and working in them to highlight His role and purpose for coming to us. The things we shall see in Acts were the norm for them and should also be the norm for us today.

Empowerment

In Acts chapter 2, we see the fulfillment of the promise Jesus made to His disciples. The Holy Spirit came on the day of Pentecost and filled them, and they began to speak in other languages as the Spirit enabled them. This created quite a commotion, as people were hearing the disciples speak fluently in their own native languages – which was impossible since none of them could have possibly known those languages.

Amid all this, some people were dismissive of them, declaring they were possibly drunk. In response to this, Peter stepped up and explained what everyone was witnessing. He stated clearly this was the fulfillment of the prophecy of Joel. God had promised long ago to pour out His Spirit, and what they were witnessing at that moment was the fulfillment of that prophecy. Peter went on to preach the good news to the crowd present, and about 3,000 people that day accepted the message and were baptized. The Holy Spirit came and immediately made His presence felt and known! He worked in power through the disciples, and thousands were able to hear the good news and come to faith in Christ.

It would not be long before what they were saying and doing would catch the attention of the rulers, elders, teachers of the law, and even the high priest. Peter and John were brought before them to give an account of what they were doing and why. Peter, who only a short time before had been fearful of them, courageously and boldly testified that the miracle they had done earlier (healing a lame man) was done in the name of Jesus. The rulers and leaders noticed the change that had come over them, which was evidence of the Holy Spirit's filling and empowerment.

At the end of the meeting, they were commanded by the rulers not to speak or teach in the name of Jesus. Rather than backing down, Peter and John told them they were not going to stop and had to obey God rather than the rulers. Their bold defiance was yet another indication of the presence and power of the Spirit at work in them.

All throughout the book of Acts, there are reports of the apostles healing many sick people and those tormented by evil spirits. Through the empowerment of the Spirit, they were able to preach the good news and perform many miraculous signs and wonders that confirmed the good news they were preaching.

Wisdom and Guidance

The Holy Spirit also constantly provided wisdom and guidance to the apostles and members of the early church. As the word began to spread beyond Jerusalem, the Holy Spirit would lead them to people and places. For example, Philip was led by the Spirit to go down a particular road. While on the road, the Holy Spirit directed him to an Ethiopian eunuch who was traveling by chariot along the road. The eunuch was on his way home after having come to Jerusalem to worship. Philip was instructed by the Spirit to go near the man and his chariot. When he did so, he heard the man reading Isaiah the prophet. He struck up a conversation with him about what he was reading and was invited up into the chariot to talk to him about it. The end result was the Ethiopian eunuch heard and believed the message about Jesus and was baptized. The Ethiopian eunuch went on his way, rejoicing, and the Spirit of the Lord suddenly took Philip away. Philip followed as the Spirit led him.

After Saul's encounter with Jesus on the road to Damascus, the Lord spoke to a man named Ananias to go visit Saul and pray for him to receive his sight again. He was told by the Lord Saul had received a vision that a man named Ananias would come and place his hands on him so he would see again. At first, Ananias objected because he had heard bad reports about Saul and how he was persecuting followers of Jesus. The Lord reassured him it would be okay, so he went. He prayed for Saul, and Saul received his sight. Saul was then baptized and became a follower of Jesus. Saul also received the filling of the Holy Spirit and began to preach the good news alongside the disciples. Since Ananias was willing to follow the Spirit's leading, he was able to be instrumental in Saul's conversion and subsequent launch into ministry.

One final example of the Holy Spirit leading the early church to people is how He led Peter to Cornelius. At that time, Peter was staying in Joppa with a man named Simon, who was a tanner and who lived by the sea. At about noon one day, Peter had gone up to the roof of the house to pray. He was getting hungry and while waiting for the food to be ready, he fell into a trance and received a vision from the Lord. The vision was repeated three times, and the Lord used the vision to prepare Peter for his next ministry assignment.

With the vision fresh in his mind, men who had been sent by Cornelius to find Peter arrived at the gate of the house where he was staying, inquiring as to whether he was there. In that moment, the Spirit said to Peter the men were looking for him and to get up, go downstairs, and not hesitate to go with them. The Spirit told him He had sent them to find him. Hearing the Spirit instruct him to go, Peter went with the men to Cornelius' house. When he finally arrived, not only was Cornelius waiting for him, but also a large group of Cornelius' family and close friends, whom he had invited to be there when Peter arrived.

As Peter entered the home, he put it all together. The vision he had been given was connected to this visit to a Gentile and his guests, also Gentiles. Normally, Peter, a devout Jew, would never consider paying a visit to a Gentile or entering the home of a Gentile. However, the Holy Spirit had made known to him this was His will, so Peter obeyed.

Cornelius shared with Peter about the vision he had received and how an angel instructed him to send men to find Peter and bring him to his house. He knew Peter had a message for him and all present, so they were there to hear all God had commanded Peter to tell them. Peter, with a new understanding given to him by the Holy Spirit, proceeded to share the good news about Jesus with all of those present. Before Peter could even finish his message, the Holy Spirit came on all who heard the message.

The same Holy Spirit who had been poured out on him on the day of Pentecost was now being poured out on these Gentiles, and they also began to speak in tongues and praise God! Realizing God was making no distinction between Jew and Gentile, Peter ordered all those present to be baptized. He ended up staying with them a few more days after this. All of this happened because Peter listened and followed the Holy Spirit and His leading to go to Cornelius and share the good news with him and his guests.

Not only did the Holy Spirit lead the early disciples to specific people, but He also led them to specific places. In Acts chapter 16, Paul and his traveling companions were trying to go to the province of Asia. The Scriptures state they had been kept by the Holy Spirit from preaching the Word there. Then, they tried to go to Bithynia in Mysia, but once again the Spirit would not allow them to do so. So instead, they passed by Mysia and ended up in Troas. The Scriptures do not state what kind of roadblocks they encountered, but it was clear enough for them to know they were not going to go where they were intending to go.

While in Troas, that very night, Paul had a vision of a man from Macedonia begging them to come to Macedonia and help them. The team got ready at once and left for Macedonia, concluding that the Spirit was directing them to go there and preach the good news. They ended up having a fruitful ministry there, which included the conversions of a woman named Lydia and her household and the jailer from the prison they were held in as well as his whole household.

While Paul was in Corinth, the Lord spoke to him, "Do not be afraid; keep on speaking, do not be silent. For I am with you and no one is going to attack or harm you, because I have many people in this city" (Acts 18:9-10). After receiving this message from the Lord, Paul stayed in Corinth for a year and a half, teaching them the word of God. For someone who was a traveling preacher and constantly on the move, without these instructions from the Lord, Paul would have moved on sooner than he did. God knew whom He had in Corinth for Paul to preach to, minister to, and teach. The Lord had him stay until the assignment He had prepared for Paul was completed.

One final example is found in Acts chapter 23. It had always been Paul's desire to make it to Rome. He shared this in his letter to the Romans (Romans 1:10). The opportunity had always eluded him, but it was always in his heart to go, - if the Lord willed it for him and made it possible. In

Acts chapter 23, Paul is in Jerusalem, having been arrested, questioned, and examined by the Jewish leaders. It would appear that Paul wasn't going anywhere anytime soon. Furthermore, even before he had gone to Jerusalem, he had received several prophetic warnings of what awaited him there – arrest, trial, and imprisonment. It was in the midst of this situation that the Lord spoke these words to Paul: "Take courage! As you have testified about me in Jerusalem, you must also testify in Rome" (Acts 23:11).

Paul's arrival in Rome would not be for some time after this, but Paul did end up in Rome. He had to stay in prison for a while and was questioned by several Roman rulers, who continued to leave him in prison even though they could not find anything wrong he did upon their examination. Frustrated with the slow and never-ending process, Paul appealed to Caesar and was granted this appeal. It was then his journey to Rome began.

The journey was a perilous one, as one of the ships he had been sailing on got shipwrecked. Despite this, Paul maintained faith and clung to hope because the Lord had already told him he would make it to Rome, and not even rough waters and a shipwreck were going to stop him from getting there. At long last, he made it there, and though imprisoned, he had a fruitful ministry there, wrote letters from there, and would eventually be martyred there. God kept His promise to Paul and enabled him to make it to Rome.

The Holy Spirit also spoke to the early church through prophets. One notable prophet in the early church whose name and ministry came up in the book of Acts was a man named Agabus. He is first encountered in Acts chapter 11, where he is mentioned as part of a group of prophets who came down from Jerusalem to Antioch. He, by the Holy

Spirit, predicted that a severe famine would spread over the entire Roman world, which happened during the reign of Claudius. Based on this prophetic word, the disciples in Antioch all decided to provide help for those living in Judea, and they sent them this gift through Barnabas and Paul.

We encounter Agabus again in Acts chapter 21, as Paul is making his way to Jerusalem. Agabus gave a prophetic word to Paul that the Jews were going to arrest him and hand him over to the Gentiles. As part of giving this prophetic message, Agabus took Paul's belt and tied his own hands and feet with it to show what the Jews would do to Paul in Jerusalem. This did not stop Paul from going, nor was it the intention of the message. The message was given to prepare Paul for what lay ahead for him in Jerusalem.

Another example of the Holy Spirit speaking to the early church through prophets is found at the beginning of Acts chapter 13. There were prophets and teachers in the church in Antioch. During a time of worship and fasting, the Holy Spirit spoke to them to set Barnabas and Saul (Paul) apart for the work to which He had called them. Once they were done fasting and praying, they placed their hands on them and sent them off on their missionary journey.

The Holy Spirit also directed the decisions the church made and the direction they took on important matters. Probably the most important of these decisions was made at a council of the leaders in Jerusalem. The question that was being raised was: Do the Gentiles need to be circumcised and required to obey the law of Moses to be saved? Some were convinced they did, and so there was disagreement among them.

Barnabas and Saul were part of that meeting, and they reported to the council all the miraculous signs and wonders God had done among the Gentiles through them and how the Gentiles everywhere they went had been converted. Peter also spoke up and relayed to them what had happened with Cornelius and all who were at his house when Peter visited them and shared the good news with them. Here are Peter's words to the council:

"Brothers, you know that some time ago God made a choice among you that the Gentiles might hear from my lips the message of the gospel and believe. God, who knows the heart, showed that He accepted them by giving the Holy Spirit to them, just as He did to us. He made no distinction between us and them, for He purified their hearts by faith. Now then, why do you try to test God by putting on the necks of the disciples a yoke that neither we nor our fathers have been able to bear? No! We believe it is through the grace of our Lord Jesus that we are saved, just as they are" (Acts 15:7-11, emphasis mine).

Having received the testimony of Barnabas, Saul, and Peter and having heard the evidence they presented of their work among the Gentiles, the council reached a conclusion. It was clear to them God wanted the gospel preached to the Gentiles and for the Gentiles to be saved. This was also in agreement with the words of the prophets in the Scriptures, which James referred to while rendering the council's verdict on the matter at hand. The decision was made they should not make it difficult for the Gentiles who were turning to God and accepting Christ and not require them to be circumcised as a condition for salvation.

Having reached this decision, they wrote a letter to the Gentiles to let them know what had been decided. They instructed them to abstain from food polluted by idols, sexual immorality, from the meat of strangled animals, and from blood. In the wording of the letter, they stated it seemed good to the Holy Spirit and them not to place any undue burden on the Gentiles who were coming to salvation through faith. In saying this, they recognized the Holy Spirit's help in reaching this decision and in enabling them to discern what His will was for them in this matter.

So, as can be seen from the accounts contained in the book of Acts, the Holy Spirit was present everywhere with them and in them. He spoke, taught, guided, empowered, and helped them in every way and at every turn. Since that was the norm for them, then it can and should be the norm for all of us!

The Scriptures vs. The Holy Spirit

Now that we've looked at the two primary ways God speaks to us, I would like to address one final issue before we move on from here. The issue is this: some people believe the Old and the New Testaments contain the complete revelation of God to man. In their minds, Genesis to Revelation encompasses everything God has spoken and ever will speak to us. Therefore, they conclude it is not necessary to seek to hear God's voice through the Holy Spirit. They will further point out that the Scriptures themselves warn us not to add to God's words or there will be serious consequences for doing so.

Is this really true? Are the Scriptures all we need? Is the Holy Spirit then not necessary? Are we faced with a situation where we have to choose one and abandon the other? Is it really an either/or question when it comes to hearing God speak to us? Can we have both the Scriptures and the Holy Spirit and listen to both speak to us or not?

I think part of the problem as stated above is a lack of understanding about how the Scriptures AND the Holy

Spirit work together in the life of a believer. Simply stated, the Scriptures contain God's agenda for us and our marching orders. When the Holy Spirit speaks to us, He teaches, leads, guides, and empowers us to carry out this agenda and these marching orders. Philippians 2:13 states "For it is God who works in you to will and to act according to His good purpose."

So, it appears, according to the Scriptures themselves, having the Scriptures alone is not enough. Just knowing what God's will and purpose is only gives us half of the equation; we also need God Himself, in the person of the Holy Spirit, living in us and working in us to carry out His will and purpose. The two complement one another and work together. They are not opposed to or against one another.

For example, the Bible instructs us to be generous and to share with those in need. The thing is, though, there are a lot of people in need, and each of us individually likely does not have the resources to help every one of them. However, with the Holy Spirit's help and guidance, we can find those whom He will bring into our path who need help and He wants us to help. Let me share a personal story that illustrates this.

Several years ago, I had a friend named George with whom I hung out twice a month. On one particular night, my friend, who was a general contractor and handyman, was paying a visit to another friend of his who was a single mom. She had just moved into a house she was renting, and she needed his help to see about hooking up a clothes dryer she had been given. It turns out the house was set up for an electric dryer, but the dryer she had received was a gas dryer. It wasn't impossible to make it work, but my friend would have to reroute some gas pipes over to where the dryer would be to make it work. So, unfortunately, it wasn't going to be as simple as just plugging in and hooking up the dryer she had.

Meanwhile, she had lots of laundry and was going to have to continue hauling it to a local laundromat to dry it. At the conclusion, my friend told her he might see if he knows someone who has an electric dryer, as this would be the simplest solution to the problem.

After our visit, the Holy Spirit spoke to me. While we were there, I felt a burden for this single mom and wanted to help her. So, the Holy Spirit told me it was what He wanted too. Then He asked me what would He do in this situation: Would He find her a beat-up old dryer, or would He provide her with a new one? The Spirit told me He wanted me to partner with Him to find and buy her a new one. He told me it was going to cost $200.

So, in my spare time, I began to research electric clothes dryers to see what they cost and to find "the one" that cost $200. Initially, my search turned up more expensive clothes dryers in the $300-$400 range. While I wasn't unwilling to spend more if needed, I knew what the Holy Spirit had shown me and had to believe there was a good dryer out there for that price.

A couple of weeks later, I called my friend up to let him know I was leaving work and coming to meet up with him to hang out. I asked where he was and if he'd had any success in finding a clothes dryer. It turned out he was at the local Home Depot and was looking at a display model dryer they were selling. When I asked him what it was going for, he told me they were selling it for $200!!

You can imagine my delight at hearing him say he had found an electric clothes dryer selling for $200. I told him that was the one because it matched what she needed and what the Holy Spirit had told me we were going to find for her. So, we purchased it along with some accessories that went with it. My friend talked them into an extra 10% off for some scuffs on the dryer itself and the final total was just a few dollars over $200 for everything.

We drove the dryer over to the friend's house and were pleased to announce to her we found her a dryer, had bought it, and were giving it to her as a gift with NO strings attached. God used us to minister to her through this gift and show her His love and care for her. I ran into her again almost 10 years later and she still remembered with great joy and gladness this simple act of kindness.

So, it is possible, desirable, and necessary to embrace both the Scriptures and the Holy Spirit to walk out God's will and purpose for our lives. We really cannot have one without the other, nor were we meant to have one without the other. In the Scriptures, we have the road map and in the Holy Spirit, we have the expert guide who can help us understand the map and point us in the right direction so we can correctly follow the map. The end result will be us living the lives God has called us to live, being a blessing to others, and bringing glory and praise to Him.

Now that we've identified the two primary ways God speaks to us, we are going to look at the different ways and means He uses to speak to us.

CHAPTER FIVE

How Does God Speak To Us? – Part II

There are two ways any message can be delivered from one person to another: directly or through a third party. If I wanted to tell you something, I could find you and tell you in person myself, call you and tell you by phone, send you an e-mail, or direct message you via text. I'm sure there are other ways too, but the point is: I am personally delivering a message to you, regardless of the means of communication I use.

What if I am unable to communicate with you directly, or maybe I simply choose to trust my message for you to another person who will relay the message on my behalf? It could be that I choose a family member or friend to deliver the message to you. I could hire a message delivery service to deliver the message to you. Either way, I am not communicating directly with you myself. I'm choosing to get my message to you through someone else, a third party to both you and me.

In the same way, when God speaks to us, sometimes He uses the direct route, which can take on a number of different forms. Other times He chooses to deliver His message to us through others whom He trusts to speak on His behalf. In this chapter, we will look at both of these to discover the ways and means God uses to speak to us.

How does God speak to us directly?

I ended the previous chapter with a story about how the Holy Spirit led me and a friend of mine to find and buy a clothes dryer for a single mom in need. How did the Holy Spirit speak to me? What was it that convinced me it was His voice and not just my imagination?

After we left the house, and even while we were there, I began to feel a burden in my heart for her and her particular need. She was pregnant at the time, and she had two younger children and two older children living there with her. I saw how many big bags full of laundry she was having to haul to a laundromat to dry. Seeing all this, my heart was moved by her need.

The burden I felt was how the Holy Spirit got my attention and became the starting point for Him to speak to me. In this instance, I did not hear an audible voice, but words and ideas entered my mind, which I attributed to Him. The crux of the message was "Find a new clothes dryer for $200."

I decided then to act on what I believed I had heard. It was in searching for and finding the dryer that fit the description of what I had "heard" that confirmed for me it was indeed the Holy Spirit who had spoken to me and directed me about this situation. I hadn't told my friend the dollar amount God had given me, so when he told me the price of the dryer he found, I knew it was the one because it was exactly as the Holy Spirit had spoken to me.

For me personally, this "inner voice" in my mind is the primary way God speaks directly to me. Since I have made it a practice over the course of the last 25 or more years of my life to ask the Holy Spirit to speak to me and to listen for His voice, I have become familiar with when He is speaking to me and have learned to recognize when it is Him and not just my own thoughts or ideas. This is the primary way He has spoken to me over the years, but it is not the only way He speaks to me. Furthermore, it is not always the primary way He speaks to other believers. There are a few different methods of communication the Lord uses to speak directly to us as revealed through the Scriptures.

Let's explore these different methods He uses, which we may encounter in our daily walk with Him.

Still Small Voice

Because the Holy Spirit lives inside of us, it's not too much of a stretch to say we also hear His voice inside of us. Sometimes it can be as short and simple as a sentence or phrase, but there are words and thoughts that "come to us" which are His voice speaking to us. A pastor friend of mine likes to say that this or that thing "pops into his head." He constantly speaks His words or ideas into our minds, and many times we are unaware it is Him!

Let me share an example from the Scriptures of this. In John chapter 2, Jesus was speaking to the Jews, who were asking Him for a sign to prove His authority to clear the temple. He said to them, "Destroy this temple, and I will raise it again in three days." No one at that time, even His disciples, understood what Jesus meant. He was referring to His own death and resurrection. In verse 22, it says after Jesus was raised from the dead, His disciples recalled what He had said and believed both the Scriptures and Jesus.

Why am I drawing attention to this? One of the things Jesus told His disciples the Holy Spirit would do is REMIND them of everything He had said to them (John 14:26). Here is a clear example of the disciples recalling something Jesus had said previously and understanding it for the first time. This is evidence of the Spirit's work in them in fulfillment of what Jesus said He would do for them. His voice inside of them helped them to connect Jesus' earlier words with His death and resurrection, and now they knew that was what Jesus had meant all along.

Jesus also promised His disciples in their moment of need, the Holy Spirit would teach them what to say and how to say it (Matthew 10:19, 20). In this specific passage, Jesus was letting them know when they were arrested because of Jesus and brought before rulers and authorities the Holy Spirit would give them what to say and would speak through them.

So, in the book of Acts when this actually happens, we see their responses are inspired by the Holy Spirit. Peter would have never defied the rulers and authorities before, but he declared to them, by the Spirit, he had to obey God rather than man when it came to proclaiming the good news. Nor was it just what he said that was given to him by the Holy Spirit, but Peter's boldness also came from the Holy Spirit and enabled him not to be intimidated by the rulers and authorities nor to back down when they ordered him to stop preaching and threatened him with punishment and prison if he did not stop. The Spirit inside of him spoke and directed him in his moment of need and gave him the perfect response to them.

Let me share another personal example of the Holy Spirit's still small voice inside of me directing and speaking to me. One Friday night many years ago, I was in my living room working on bills. I was just finishing up and about to put everything away when a thought entered my mind, "Take your checkbook with you tonight." I was going to visit a church that was having their weekly Friday night service, and normally I would not take my checkbook in such a situation. Still, I believed what I heard was the Holy Spirit, so I obeyed and expected Him to direct me while I was at the service that night.

After worship, they took their regular offering, but I did not feel directed to give. Then, a little while later, they decided to take up a missions offering, but I still did not feel directed to give. While they were taking up their missions offering, they asked a young man in their congregation who was a rap artist to come up and share one of his songs with everyone. After he was finished and the missions offering was collected, the pastor came up and stood with the young man. Rather than just thanking him for the song and dismissing him to his seat, the pastor decided that anyone who wanted to give an offering to the young man in support of his music could do so at that time. At that moment, I got the green light from the Holy Spirit to give and made out a check to the young man. I was thrilled I had taken the earlier thought to heart and now knew it was the Holy Spirit speaking and directing me.

Further, I was excited to recognize when and to whom He was leading me to give. In all of this, the Holy Spirit's voice inside of me spoke to me and then further guided and directed me at just the right moment.

Audible Voice

Along with His voice inside of us, God also at times has spoken in an audible voice. The Old and New Testaments record examples of this. In the Old Testament, when God spoke to the people of Israel at Mount Sinai, the Scriptures record they heard "The sound of words but saw no form; there was only a voice" (Deuteronomy 4:12). It is clear from this passage God's voice was an audible voice they were able to hear with their physical ears. Unfortunately, when they heard His voice and saw the display of fire, black clouds, and deep darkness, they were frightened to the point where they begged Moses to ask God not to speak to them anymore! They asked God to tell Moses everything and then have Moses report to them what God had said. God agreed to this at that time, but His sincere desire then and now is for all people to be able to hear His voice without a mediator.

The New Testament also records a number of instances when God spoke with an audible voice. Among these instances are the following: at the baptism of Jesus (Matthew 3:13-17), the transfiguration of Jesus (Matthew 17:1-8), once when Jesus was foretelling His death (John 12:23-30), and at Paul's conversion (Acts 9:1-7). In the first three instances mentioned here, the voice spoke for the benefit of those present and either confirmed what Jesus was saying or confirmed His identity as the Son of God. In the instance with Paul, Jesus himself appeared to Paul and spoke to Paul for his benefit, and the others there with him were able to hear the sound of the voice speaking.

Though there are not many instances in which God spoke to mankind in an audible voice, the fact He did, and they are recorded in the Scriptures show He has done so, and it is possible He could if He chose to do so. We must also remember God has spoken to mankind in an audible voice through Jesus, as the Word became flesh and dwelt among us. God's Son is the ultimate example of God speaking to us in an audible voice. Where, when, and with whom He uses this direct method of communication is entirely up to Him.

Visions and Dreams

One very common way God speaks and has spoken to people is through visions and dreams. The simplest explanation for the difference between these two is visions typically occur when a person is awake, and dreams normally occur when a person is asleep. A vision can be seen by the natural eyes or by the mind's eyes (eyes of our heart or spirit).

There are many examples in the Scriptures of people receiving visions from God as a form He used to speak directly to them. The major prophets – Isaiah, Jeremiah, and Ezekiel – all had visions from God at the time God called them to be prophets (see Isaiah 6, Jeremiah 1, and Ezekiel 1 for those accounts). When the prophet Elisha was surrounded by the Aramean army, the Lord enabled his servant to see the heavenly army that surrounded the Aramean army in the form of horses and chariots of fire (II Kings 6:8-17). The prophet Daniel also received visions from God about things to come (see Daniel 8 and 10). Moses, Aaron, Nadab, Abihu, and the seventy elders of Israel all were enabled to see God Himself! Towards the end of the Old Testament, the prophet Joel prophesied that one day God would pour out His Spirit and all people would be enabled to see visions (Joel 2:28).

Consistent with the Old Testament and with Joel's prophecy, people in the New Testament also experienced seeing visions. As mentioned before, Peter, prior to visiting Cornelius, received a vision from God that showed him God accepted the Gentiles and not to consider them unclean or unacceptable any longer (Acts 10, with Peter's explanation in Acts 11). The apostle Paul claimed to have received visions from the Lord (2 Corinthians 12). While his purpose for bringing this up to the Corinthians was to emphasize to them what the true marks of an apostle were versus what they thought the true marks of an apostle ought to be, he nonetheless pointed out he had received visions from the Lord. Finally, the book of Revelations contains visions God gave to John about the realities in heaven, the end times, and things to come.

It is noticeable in these instances recorded, with the exception of Elisha's servant, that visions were given to prophets and apostles. Yet because of Joel's prophecy and the emphasis on God pouring out His Spirit on all flesh, it is right to say God uses visions to communicate with all people now, not just prophets and apostles. It has always been God's intention to communicate directly with us and not just through mediators like prophets and apostles. Visions are definitely one way He does this.

Let me share a quick personal example. On my second trip to South Asia, we traveled to remote villages to show the Jesus film and to do evangelism. In one of the villages, we made a quick visit to a small church. While they were singing a worship song, I had a vision of Jesus dancing with delight as they sang and worshipped. I shared this vision with them and encouraged them that Jesus was delighted by their worship. During the remainder of this trip, God gave me a message on worship I was able to preach and share on 3 different occasions. Looking back, it was clear to me these things were connected and were part of what God wanted to show me and communicate through me during the trip.

Along with visions, there are many examples in the Scriptures where God used dreams to communicate with people. In the Old Testament, God revealed Himself to Jacob through a dream when he was at Bethel (Genesis 28). His son, Joseph, received a dream that revealed his role as a ruler in the future (Genesis 37). God also gave dreams to people in Joseph's path – Pharaoh's cupbearer and baker as well as Pharaoh himself – and enabled Joseph to interpret their dreams for them (Genesis 40 and 41). Amazingly, it was through interpreting Pharaoh's dream that Joseph's dream of becoming a ruler became a reality. Finally, God spoke to King Nebuchadnezzar through dreams and used Daniel to interpret those dreams for him (Daniel 2 and 4).

In the New Testament, God spoke to Joseph, Jesus' earthly father, through dreams, giving him warnings and directions (Matthew 1:20-25 and 2:13-23). God also spoke to the Magi through a dream not to return to King Herod (Matthew 2:12). As part of Joel's prophecy referred to earlier, God promised to enable people to dream dreams when He would pour out His Spirit on all people. So. it is reasonable to expect God will use dreams to speak to us today.

Once again, let me share a personal example. When I was 15 years old, I had a dream I was preaching in the Soviet Union (it was 1987 and there was still a Soviet Union). Because of this dream, I concluded God was calling me to be a missionary to the Soviet Union. From that point on, I set my sights on going into the ministry and preparing to be a missionary. I went to college to study the Bible and missions, and after college, I went to San Francisco and helped start a church there.

During my time in San Francisco, our lead pastor had some missionary friends come and visit us and share what they were doing. It turned out that these missionary friends were working in a country called Kyrgyzstan, which was in the former Soviet Union! When I learned this, I knew I had to connect with them and share with them my dream of preaching there and the calling God had given me in 1987 (I crossed paths with them in 1998). The lead pastor, knowing this, invited me to join them after the night service for dinner. I established a connection with them at that time and heard more about what they were doing, and we agreed to stay in touch.

About a year later, they reached out to me and invited me to come to Kyrgyzstan to minister. There was a Bible College near where they were staying. The college was training pastors and leaders to go back and work in the surrounding nations (including Kyrgyzstan). Students hailed from Azerbaijan, Kazakhstan, Uzbekistan, and Kyrgyzstan. The courses were a month long, so I was invited to come be a guest professor and teach a course at the college as well as take advantage of any preaching opportunities in local churches that presented themselves to me. Without hesitation, I accepted their invitation and set a date with them to come teach and minister in February of 2000.

My time spent there would be the only time I've been to the former Soviet Union, at least this far into my life. The Lord has not led me or enabled me to go back yet, but I hope to do so and believe I will someday return and minister there again. I know the dream I had as a teenager and the opportunity that came about a dozen years later were connected. God indeed had spoken to me through a dream and at the right time, he brought to reality what he showed me in the dream!

The Scriptures and Jesus

The words and messages of the Scriptures were originally delivered to a particular audience at a specific time and place in history. Similarly, the words of Jesus while He lived His earthly life were spoken to the people Jesus encountered during the time span in which He ministered and carried out His Father's will. They were the ones God spoke to directly when those messages were first delivered. This means we today are the indirect recipients of what God spoke in the past through the Scriptures and Jesus.

However, God's words are eternal, and He intended for them to apply not just to those who originally heard them but also to the generations of people to follow who were not present when He originally spoke those words the first time around. When God speaks today, He will speak these same words to us afresh and anew, applying them to us as He did to those who first heard them. For example, He will remind us of promises made long ago in the Scriptures that apply to us here and now. His Word is living and active, and He wants His words to come alive to us today and bring life to us as they did to those in the past. His word never becomes obsolete regardless of how long ago He originally declared it.

As an example of this, consider what Peter said to the crowd on the day of Pentecost when the Holy Spirit was poured out and the group of believers began to speak in tongues. People were mocking them and accusing them of being drunk. The Holy Spirit helped Peter to make a connection between what was now happening and the words of the prophet Joel from many centuries before. When Peter declared "This is that" – he was pointing to what was originally said in the past and declaring it was being fulfilled in their midst in the present time. The words of the prophet did not die with him; since they were God's words, they were alive and well and waiting for the time when they would be fulfilled – which was at that moment.

Peter went on to say this promise which was now being fulfilled in their midst would continue to be fulfilled in future generations as well (see Acts 2:39). The present fulfillment of this prophetic promise was just the beginning. Even roughly 2000 years removed from the original day of Pentecost outpouring, any time God pours out His Spirit today, we can confidently say as Peter did "This is what was spoken by the prophet Joel."

What is true about the Scriptures is also true about the words of Jesus. The Scriptures record instances when God brought the words of Jesus back to mind when He spoke to different people. One notable example of this is when Peter was at Cornelius' house and the Holy Spirit was poured out on all of those present. When later recounting the story of what happened to circumcised believers who objected to him going into Cornelius' house, Peter told them as the Spirit was being poured out on those present, he remembered what the Lord Jesus had said. Jesus had said, "John baptized with water, but you will be baptized with the Holy Spirit." These words of Jesus came fresh to Peter's mind as he witnessed the outpouring of the Holy Spirit on Cornelius and those present at his house. In that moment, God was declaring Jesus' words afresh to Peter, showing what He said before applied now.

In keeping with this, Jesus himself had told them this would happen. In John 16:14, Jesus told His disciples the Holy Spirit would "Bring glory to Me by taking from what is Mine and making it known to you." In the instances recorded in the Scriptures where this takes place, the Holy Spirit reminded the disciples of Jesus' words and gave them an understanding of those words they did not have when they heard them originally. Though Jesus had left them to return to His Father in heaven, the Holy Spirit would draw upon the things Jesus had for them – including His words to them – and apply them afresh and anew in their lives.

This same opportunity exists for us today. When God speaks to us, He will declare His words from the Scriptures and the words Jesus spoke long ago afresh and anew to us. God is not above repeating Himself, especially when what He has to say is still valid and relevant. He will not only speak those words to us again, but He will give us revelation, knowledge, and understanding of what they mean and how they apply to us now.

As a personal example, I recall a time I was feeling particularly anxious and discouraged. In some areas, I thought I should be further along in my spiritual growth than I actually was. In my own frustration with myself, I was worried that perhaps God was also frustrated with me too. The Holy Spirit spoke to me and encouraged me through Philippians 1:6, where Paul tells the Philippians he is confident that God, who started a good work in them, would be faithful to finish and complete that work until the day of Christ Jesus. In the same way, the Holy Spirit encouraged me. He knew I was a work in progress. He was not done with me yet. He was still working on and in me and would continue to do so until He finished what He had started in me.

This brought me great encouragement and relief, especially because the Holy Spirit not only spoke to me in my time of need but also because He employed the Scriptures to confirm and reinforce what He was saying to me. He took the words of Paul, written centuries before to the Philippian church, and spoke them to me afresh and anew, applying them to how I was feeling at that time. His word is alive and well, and He will continue to make use of it constantly when He speaks to us today.

How Does God Speak to Us Via Third Party?

There are also times when God chooses to send messengers on His behalf to deliver His messages to us. He does not choose just anyone to do this. He chooses those He knows He can trust to deliver His messages for Him. Not only that, but He also chooses those who will not alter or garble the message He has given them to deliver. The responsibility of the messenger is both to deliver and safeguard the message they have been entrusted to deliver. So, who are these 3rd party messengers?

Angels

In studying the Old and New Testaments, there are a number of examples where God spoke to mankind through angels. One messenger angel whose name is specifically mentioned in Scripture is Gabriel. In Daniel chapters 8 and 9, he appeared to Daniel to bring him understanding of the visions he had been given and to explain their meaning. Gabriel is also the messenger angel who was sent to Zechariah, John the Baptist's father, and to Mary, the mother of Jesus (see Luke chapter 1).

Paul also mentions God used angels to give the law Moses received for the people of Israel (Galatians 3:19). In Hebrews chapter 1, the writer calls them ministering spirits who are sent to serve those who will inherit salvation. So, it should come as no surprise to us angels are involved in all God is doing here on earth and they have important roles to play in God's great plan for the ages.

With regard to hearing from God through angels, the Scriptures' main emphasis is to warn us not all "spirits" are from God and to test the spirits to determine if they are from God or not. Paul goes so far as to say in his letter to the Galatians if anyone, including an angel from heaven, preached a gospel different than the one he had already presented they should be eternally condemned for doing this. This is so critical to Paul that he says it twice just for emphasis (Galatians 1:6-9).

John in his first letter instructs believers NOT to believe every spirit but to test the spirits to see whether they are from God. In this context, John is specifically addressing the teaching of some who denied Jesus had come in the flesh, which John knew was not true since John had been with Jesus when He was in the flesh. By testing the spirits, the believers would be able to recognize who was from God and who was from the deceiver. (I John 4:1-6).

Essentially, any teaching that alters the gospel message or makes Jesus less than fully human or less than fully God is a teaching not from God. Any teaching that does not lead us to Christ as Savior and Lord, to Christ as the means of forgiveness for our sins and source of eternal life, to Christ the one who reconciles us to God and brings us into His kingdom and into the royal family, is not from God. Since God has seen fit to give us the Scriptures and the Holy Spirit, who is the Spirit of truth and the one who leads us into all truth, we have what we need from God to stay in the truth and recognize and avoid all that might look or sound good on the surface but ultimately is in error and not from Him.

God wants us to be wise and discerning and has given us what we need to be both. It's up to us then to take what we hear – even from a so-called angel of God – and test it by what we already know to be true. If it passes the test, great! If it does not pass the test, the message and the messenger ought to be rejected.

Other People

One of the great things about God is He does not expect us to go through this life alone. Even from the very beginning, when He created Adam and Eve, God determined it was not good for man to be alone. We were created to be part of a community and contribute to the life of that community as well as benefit from the contributions of others into that community. As believers, we are the body of Christ, and as each part does its part, all parts are built up and receive what they need to grow and mature. This is all by God's perfect design.

As it relates to hearing God's voice, we not only can hear from God for ourselves, but we can also hear from God for others. We can hear His voice speaking to us through our fellow believers. God accomplishes this in a number of different ways. First of all, God has set in place for the church apostles, prophets, evangelists, pastors, and teachers (Ephesians 4:11). Their primary job is to prepare God's people for works of service. One of the ways they do this is through preaching and teaching the Scriptures and relying on the Holy Spirit to speak through them as they preach and teach. In this way, the Holy Spirit speaks to us through their ministries, and we are built up, encouraged, and equipped for service as God intended.

One mistake I have seen people make, though, is they will take what they hear from church leaders as God's voice to them but not pursue trying to hear God's voice on their own. Either they do not know they can hear God's voice for themselves, don't know how to hear His voice, or simply lack the confidence they can hear God's voice in the same way their pastors and leaders do. If I accomplish nothing else with this book, I hope in writing this I dispel this myth. Yes, all believers can hear from God, can learn how to hear from Him, and can grow in confidence in hearing from Him by recognizing how He speaks to us and developing an open heart and listening ear.

This is not to downplay the role of the leaders God has given us. Thank God, He has given us leaders and overseers in the body of Christ! We should certainly honor those whose work it is to lead the church and pray they may do it in such a way that both pleases God who called them and imparts life to those they are called to serve. Still, God's will and design is each and every member is a contributor to the body of Christ.

We all have one and the same Spirit. The Holy Spirit inside of every believer is the SAME Spirit in our pastors and other leaders. Just as He enables them to hear from Him and do the work He has called them to do, He enables each and every believer also to hear from Him and do the work He has called them to do.

The Scriptures confirm all of this. In I Corinthians 12:4-6, Paul wrote these words:

> "There are different kinds of gifts, but the same Spirit. There are different kinds of service, but the same Lord. There are different kinds of working, but the same God works all of them in all men."

Paul lists a number of spiritual gifts the Spirit gives to all believers for the benefit of all. Among them are speaking gifts – the message of wisdom, the message of knowledge, prophecy, speaking in tongues, and interpretation of tongues. All of these are from the Spirit and are given as He sees fit to all believers within the community of believers. Potentially, everyone equally has access to them and can operate in any of these speaking gifts.

A couple of chapters later, in I Corinthians 14, Paul isolates the gift of prophecy and expounds on its importance within the body of Christ. He instructs the believers as to its proper use in their meetings and gatherings. Essentially, he tells them all to eagerly desire the gifts of the Spirit, especially prophecy. Prophecy's purpose is to strengthen, encourage, and comfort others in the body of Christ.

Since this should be the aim or purpose of their gatherings, then they should want to operate in gifts that accomplish this goal. Paul further says if several believers have a prophetic word or message, they can all take turns sharing what God has given them for the rest. Paul never wanted the gifts to be hindered in their midst; he did, however, want believers to remember the purpose behind the gifts and to operate in those gifts in an orderly way.

Some of the greatest messages from God I have ever received were not from pastors in pulpits. I have received great encouragement and comfort from other believers who simply heard from God and spoke to me what He gave them for me. I have also been blessed to have opportunities to do the same for others. Sometimes the most impactful messages in our lives don't come from the weekly church service but from a phone conversation or a talk over coffee.

With this in mind, we should all be encouraged to know we can hear from God for each other, and He can use us to make a difference in each other's lives if we will simply hear what He is saying and share it with those who need to hear it.

In this chapter, we have explored the ways God speaks to us directly and how He also uses others to deliver His messages to us. Mere words alone are not the only way He communicates with us. Let's now look at another vital and important way He speaks to all of us: by His actions.

CHAPTER SIX

How Does God Speak To Us? – Part III

There was a man who had two sons. He went to the first and said, "Son, go and work today in the vineyard." "I will not," he answered, but later he changed his mind and went.

Then the father went to the other son and said the same thing. He answered, "I will, sir," but he did NOT go. Which of the two DID what his father wanted? (Matthew 21:28-31)

Though the first son told his father he would not go and work in the vineyard, he changed his mind and went. The second son said he would go but did not follow through and actually do it. It was the first son who did what his father wanted – even though, initially, his words would indicate he wasn't going to do so. By his actions, he demonstrated his willingness and obedience to do what his father had told him to do.

There is a familiar saying, "Actions speak louder than words." This is true of God and how He speaks to us. He speaks to us by how He works in our lives, in the lives of others, and in the world around us. He speaks to us by all the things He does for us. He is not merely someone who says the right words – He backs those words up with actions. He doesn't just tell us a thousand times a day He loves us – He acts in ways that SHOW us He loves us. He doesn't make empty promises – He acts to keep His promises and fulfill them in our lives. Everything He says He backs up with actions that agree with His words.

The greatest action God has taken on our behalf – sending His Son Jesus to die for our sins and to become the Way for us to be reconciled to God – speaks volumes. This action plan God put into effect in the fullness of time speaks of His great love for us, His great mercy and grace, His kindness, His favor, and His great desire to be in a relationship with us. So, what other actions can we see God doing in our lives that speak to us and demonstrate His interest and love for us?

He Forgives

For one thing, He forgives us of our sins. In Psalm 32, David praises God's forgiveness and shows us what it was like for him before and after He was forgiven. Before he received God's forgiveness, David was miserable and weighed down. Then David confessed his sins to God and quit hiding them from God, and God forgave all of David's sins. The Psalm is a song of praise to God for the forgiveness David received and the life-giving effects it had on him.

I have also found this to be true. The story I shared at the beginning of this book highlighted how burdened I was by guilt for stealing a candy bar out of my teacher's desk and how when I finally accepted God's forgiveness, the burden was removed. At different times in my life, I have been weighed down with a guilty conscience from my own sins. When I finally wised up and confessed my sins to God, I received His forgiveness and felt the weight that had been pushing down on me lifted off me. It's as if the clouds dispersed entirely and the sun and blue skies were there once again. Since God made a way through Jesus' death on our behalf for us to be forgiven of all of our sins, we can not only receive that forgiveness but can also feel its effects on us when He acts to forgive us.

He Sets Us Free

Another way God acts that speaks to us is He sets us free. Freedom has two parts. God sets us free from the compulsion and control of sin. He sets us free to do the things that are good and right. Paul says in Galatians 5:1 where the Spirit of the Lord is, there is freedom. God acts in us to free us from all that holds us down and holds us back so we can live the lives He has purposed and destined for us to live.

Take the apostle Peter for example. Here was a guy who displayed bravado when Jesus told him he would deny Him three times. Peter adamantly asserted he would never do that to Jesus and was ready to be arrested and die with Him. But when the time came, Peter's fears crept to the surface and his words and actions didn't measure up to his previous promises to Jesus.

However, all was not lost with Peter. After Jesus' resurrection, Peter would be filled with the Holy Spirit on the day of Pentecost and boldly proclaim Jesus was the Christ. Opposition would come in the form of being arrested and questioned by the religious leaders, but that did not make Peter revert to his formerly fearful ways. Peter stood up to them and told them he had to obey God and not them.

Peter continued to preach the good news and risk being arrested or worse. Gone were the fears that had plagued him before; no longer did he have to manufacture courage on his own. The Holy Spirit inside of him had set him free from fear and replaced the fear in him with boldness. As Peter depended on the Holy Spirit, He was able to do what he was called to do, having been set free from what held him back in the past.

As God has worked in my life to set me free, I have discovered this is a work He does that is ongoing in our lives. God will identify an area in which He wants to bring freedom, and as I say "Yes" to Him and walk it out, I discover I can do things I could not do before. Over time, I become more like Him in that area.

Of the many areas where I have seen Him do this, the one area I want to highlight is His work to uproot selfishness from me. This work is by no means complete, but as I have allowed God access to this part of me, He has transformed and enabled me to put others ahead of myself. I have seen this happen especially with my children. Children will either make or break you when it comes to selfishness. My children want and need things constantly – whether it's my attention, my time, my help, or some tangible thing – my children look to me for these things. Much of the time, for me to give them what they want or need requires I put aside what I want or need in order to serve them and provide good things for them.

As I have done this consistently over time, I have discovered not just I can do this but I enjoy doing it. I love seeing my children happy and fulfilled because I took time and made them a priority. By yielding to God's work in my life in this area – being selfless and prioritizing others have become a part of who I am and something I can do with ease and delight. This is true freedom, and I am thankful God has not only taught me what freedom in Him looks like, but He also works in me to make that freedom a growing and ever-increasing reality.

He Heals

God is also a healer, and another way He speaks to us is by healing us. His healing can take on many forms – physical healing for sure, but also mental and emotional healing as well. God can and does heal relationships too. I have known a number of couples who had gotten divorced, and then found healing in their individual lives, which led to healing in their relationship, which led to them getting remarried to one another!

The Scriptures are filled with accounts of God displaying His healing power. Jesus healed everyone who came to Him. The apostles were empowered by the Holy Spirit to perform many miracles, including miraculous healings. Paul also mentions gifts of healing and the ability to do miracles among the gifts the Spirit distributes to the church. Because of this, we should not be surprised to find these gifts in operation today.

When God heals, it communicates many things to us. The greatest thing His healing communicates is: He is powerful and willing to use His power to enact good for us. In one encounter Jesus had with a man with leprosy, the man said to Jesus, "Lord, if you are willing, you can make me clean." In response to this, Jesus reached out and touched the man saying, "I am willing, be clean!" (Matthew 8:1-4) In healing this man, we see God's power combined with a willingness to use that power to heal. I am convinced His power is still available to us today, to all who believe and will ask Him in faith. I am also persuaded He is just as willing now as He was then, and He longs to display His love in our lives through His healing power and touch.

Since He still has the power to answer and willingness to act, it would seem the onus lies on us to believe and ask. The reason I say this is because there are those who ask why we don't see more miracles or healings these days, especially if these things were the norm for the apostles and the early church. The Scriptures clearly say we have not because we ask not. So, if these things are really true about God – that He has the power to heal and the willingness to do so, then it is up to us to take Him up on what He is making available to us. When we decide to do that, to give Him the opportunity to do what He said He would do, then we will see more of the miraculous and more demonstrations of His power in our lives.

Before moving on, let me share a story of God's healing power I was a part of firsthand. Many years ago, I was a member of a church called The Mission. I had received training and joined the church's prayer team. Once a month on a Sunday night, we would have healing services and pray for the sick and hurting.

After some brief worship and a few encouraging words, we opened up the service to pray for those who had come for prayer. I was approached by a friend of mine named John. He had a neck injury from many years before that had never fully gotten better. He had to see a chiropractor regularly for his neck.

As I began to pray for him for healing, he noticed some improvement but not fully. As we continued to pray, hoping to see complete healing, John noticed the pain kept moving away from where I put my hand. If I put my hand in the spot where it was hurting, that spot would feel better, but then the pain would shift to a different spot in his neck. The pain was "moving" – kind of going back and forth between two spots.

We asked for the Lord's guidance in this. John recalled having gotten treatment in the past in a way he felt may not have pleased the Lord. He confessed this to God and asked for forgiveness for it. Right after he did that, we prayed for him once more, and the pain totally and completely left!

John tested his neck out for a few moments just to be sure, but he felt no pain, and no amount of turning his neck one way or another brought him any pain! We were convinced God had completely healed him. A few months later, our senior pastor brought John up to the stage in the middle of worship to share testimony of his healing. He had gone back to his chiropractor, who, after having looked him over, was amazed to see John in such a healthy state. John reported since that time, the injury to his neck was no more and had not returned. God had healed him completely and permanently!

He Protects

Another way God speaks to us through His actions is He protects us. The Scriptures are filled with God's saving and rescuing acts on behalf of His people. The entire story of Exodus shows many instances in which God protected His people from the plagues He sent on Egypt. All of this culminated in one final rescue as the Israelites crossed the Red Sea on dry ground and then Pharaoh and his army were submerged in that same sea once all of Israel had crossed safely to the other side.

The Scriptures also record many instances in which God protected individuals. From the same exodus story, we see how God protected Moses at a time when all Israelite male children were ordered to be killed. The story of King

David's life is filled with many instances of God's deliverance and protection from dangers and enemies.

Many of David's psalms are songs of praise to God for His protection and rescue out of all his life's perils. We can also see God's rescue in the lives of Shadrach, Meshach, and Abednego from Nebuchadnezzar's fiery furnace and Daniel from his lion's den. From all of this, it can be said God does step in to protect, save, and rescue us and show Himself to us in the midst of potentially harmful and dangerous situations, some even life-threatening.

I do want to share one personal example of God's protection that has always stood out to me. Many years ago, I was driving to work one morning when my car began to act up. For no explicable reason, it began to idle at 4,000 - 5,000 RPMs, and no matter what I did, it would not stop. I hit the gas pedal a number of times and that didn't work. I pulled off to the shoulder, turned the car off, and waited a few minutes. Afterward, I restarted the car, and it went back again to the abnormally high idle.

At this point, I determined something was definitely wrong and my car was unfit to drive. So, I turned the car off again and proceeded to call for a tow truck. Minutes later, I was riding with the tow truck driver back into town to take my car to a mechanic who could assess what this strangle idling problem was and fix it.

A few hours later, I got a call from the mechanic stating the idling problem had stopped and not shown any sign of returning. That was a relief. However, while on the test drive, the brakes seemed to go out, and the brake pedal was going all the way to the floor. They were barely able to stop the car safely. Since they didn't work on the brakes, but there was a brake shop around the corner from their shop, I asked them if they would take my vehicle to that shop and drop it off. I called the brake shop and asked them inspect this brake issue that seemed to have appeared from out of nowhere.

A little while later that afternoon, they called and let me know one of the brake lines had broken and needed to be replaced. The failed brake line was the reason the other shop had difficulty slowing and stopping my vehicle. They were able to do the repair that afternoon, and I was able to get my car back at the end of the day after work.

What the Lord showed me in all of this was He knew the brake line was going to fail and if I had continued driving to work, I could have lost the ability to slow down and stop my car on the highway and most likely would have been in an accident that could have seriously injured me and others. So, while the unusually high idling problem wasn't the real problem and turned out to be nothing at all, God knew what the real problem was and used that situation to get me to pull off the road. I honestly and truly believe in all of this He protected me and kept me safe.

What makes this stand out even more to me is I was in the midst of a time in my life where I felt worthless and like my life didn't matter. Honestly, I had a very bleak outlook on my life during that period of time and was really questioning whether my life was worth living or whether I was of any value to God or to others. So, when all of this happened and the Lord showed me how He protected me from harm that day, it wasn't just He protected me. Through His protection that day, He made it abundantly clear my life mattered to Him, and I was valuable to Him.

He Provides For Our Needs

Yet another way God speaks to us through His actions is He provides for our needs. We all have many and varied needs. At the most basic level, we need water, food, clothing, and shelter. We have physical needs, financial and material needs, mental, emotional, and spiritual needs, and social and relational needs. I'm certain there are probably other needs we have too. The good news is God knows ALL of our needs and ALL we need. He is not unaware of how He made us and what we need to function on a daily basis. Not only does He know our needs, He has the power and the resources to provide for ALL of our needs in adequate and abundant supply.

Sadly, at times we are all a little too focused on our needs. In some cases, this focus turns into anxiety, worry, and even fear. When that happens, our tendency is to take matters into our own hands, and when we do, we lose sight of the One who sees us, who knows our needs, and who cares for us.

It is at these times we need to be reminded of the words of Jesus in Matthew 6:25-34. As Jesus was addressing the multitudes who had gathered to listen to Him teach, He spoke to them about this issue of unhealthy preoccupation and worry about one's needs. He reminded them God feeds the birds and clothes the flowers of the fields, neither of whom expend the effort that mankind expends to get those same things. Jesus then made the connection if God does these things for birds and flowers, how much more would He do them for His people, His dear children whom He loves.

Jesus also demonstrated this very thing on a number of occasions by performing provision miracles. Perhaps the most notable of these was the feeding of more than five thousand people when all they had on hand was five small loaves of bread and two small fishes – barely enough food to feed the young boy who brought these to the disciples and Jesus. This miracle was a profound illustration of Jesus' teaching that God would provide for our needs, even when it was not clear where the provision would come from or how it would be done. Through this miraculous sign, Jesus made it abundantly clear those who look to God to provide for them will have their needs met and will be free to put their focus on more important things – the most important being Jesus and His kingdom.

I have seen God provide all of the things I have mentioned and more time and time again throughout my life. He has always come through, so I have lacked no good thing. Truly I can say He is my shepherd and I want for nothing. I would like to share one example of how I have seen Him speak to me by providing for me.

When I was a pastor helping plant a church in San Francisco, there was a six-month period where I was able to devote myself to the ministry full-time. Up until that point, I was working a full-time job for income while giving my extra time on evenings and weekends to the work of the church. I did this for the first three-plus years of my time there.

One thing we had done with the church building we were renting was to create rooms and space for people to live at the church building. We created space for staff and students at our discipleship school. One of the staff members felt called to leave and return to Los Angeles to get married and take a position at a church down there. With his room vacated, I saw an opportunity to quit my job, move out of my apartment, move into the open room in the church, and devote myself full-time to the ministry. The room would be rent-free, and my expenses as a single person would be minimal. I was able to use financial support from family and friends to cover my needs.

I must say the 6 months of being able to be full-time in ministry was like a dream come true for me. Unfortunately, at the end of the summer, our lead pastor announced we would be vacating our lease of the building and searching for a new building. Everyone who lived there was given this notice and encouraged to find jobs and housing as soon as possible. The news came as a shock to all of us, and for me, it was also sad and disappointing because I was truly enjoying the experience of just being in ministry.

Nevertheless, like the others, I had to begin the search for a job and an apartment. Before my search began, as I was praying about all of these new developments, I heard the Lord speak to me he would indeed provide a new job and apartment for me as well as an office for me. This last thing was not something I was asking for or even thinking about, but I was convinced this is what I heard God say to me. So, I expressed my thanksgiving for His promises and was intrigued to see how all of this would unfold in the days ahead.

Within a couple of days of the announcement, a friend of mine at church, who worked in a hotel in downtown San Francisco, told me she thought there were some job openings available within the small hotel chain her hotel was a part of and encouraged me to look into it. So, I reached out to the manager of one of these hotels that had a front desk clerk opening available and set up an interview. At the interview, he hired me right on the spot and wanted to get me working as soon as possible. This was maybe two or three days after the initial announcement. I checked this off of my list and turned my focus to the apartment search.

One of the guys who was a student and also lived in the church building asked me if I wanted to be roommates and find a place together. I had gotten to know him over the course of living with him in the church building, and he seemed like a good guy and someone who would make a good roommate. Also, he worked in construction as a carpenter and was already offered his old job back. I said yes to his offer, and so began the apartment search with him. About four or five days after the initial announcement, he had found a two-bedroom place available and had talked to the landlady and seen it. She liked him and wanted to rent the place to me and him, but she wanted to meet me first and get my information. His credit was not as good as mine, so if my credit numbers were appealing to her, she would agree to lease to us.

When I saw the place, I loved it and really hoped we would get it. After supplying her with both our employment details and credit details, she informed us a few days later she would rent the place to us. This was maybe ten days at most after the initial announcement we had to vacate the church building. I was so excited to see God move so quickly and favorably on my behalf in this time of need.

What about the "office?" To reiterate, the thought that I "needed" an office had not crossed my mind nor can I say it was my idea. Yet I was certain about what I heard God say to me. So, about a month later, I was talking to my mom. She had been talking to my uncle, who had asked her if I had a computer and a desk. This seemed unusual to me that he would ask her that, but being that I did not have these things, I told her I did not. I also asked her why he would be asking her about that. Furthermore, I had not mentioned to anyone about what God had spoken to me – not family members or friends – no one at all.

She proceeded to tell me some of his stocks had earned some dividends and he wanted to use some of that money to help me if I needed it. He wanted to give me enough to pay for a new computer, a desk, and office supplies. I was speechless. This was above and beyond what I had asked for and what I thought I needed, yet God saw a need I didn't even know I had and provided for me in a way I never saw coming.

It turned out that computer and desk would help me in the short term and the long term. A little over a year later, I would leave San Francisco completely, and I spent several months getting ready to go overseas to teach a class at a Bible college. Having the computer and all of the office supplies were essential in helping me prepare all of the course materials I would take with me to teach. So not only did God meet a need I didn't know I had, but He also had the foresight to see beyond my immediate circumstances and provide for me things I would need down the road.

In watching all of this play out before my eyes, I saw God move on my behalf to provide and take care of me in all things. I was impressed and amazed at the speed at which He did things and the thoroughness with which He covered me. Before I could even begin to worry or wonder if and how He would do things, they were already done. Most of all, because He did all of these things and provided for me so completely, I was able to keep my focus on Him and prioritize the things that were far more important. Jesus' words rang true: put His kingdom first, and He will provide and take care of all the rest.

He Directs Our Paths

Another way God speaks to us through His actions is by directing our paths. The Scriptures state a very clear promise to all of us: if we will trust the Lord with our whole hearts and not lean on our own understandings (or misunderstandings) but acknowledge the Lord in all things, He will direct our paths (see Proverbs 3:5-6). Sometimes He tells us the way, but many times He SHOWS us the way.

Let us consider the example of Jonah: The fact is, Jonah KNEW where God wanted him to go and what God wanted him to do there. Jonah, however, chose to flee in the opposite direction. He boarded a boat and tried to sail far away from the destination God had in mind for Him. In response to this, God sent a violent storm that nearly destroyed the ship he was on and all of the passengers along with it. Once they discovered why the storm had been sent and who was responsible, they proceeded to throw Jonah overboard. Amazingly, after they did this, the storm stopped, and everything became calm once more.

Then, as the story goes, after Jonah is thrown overboard, He is swallowed by a large fish. He remained inside the large fish for three days and nights. When the time came, the large fish "deposited" Jonah back onto the shore. Realizing God was not permitting him to flee from the responsibility he had been given, Jonah, at last, decided to go to Nineveh. God's actions communicated to Jonah there was nowhere he could flee where God could not follow and re-direct him into the path He had ordained for him.

Also consider the example of the apostles in the book of Acts. Unlike Jonah, they were trying to obey and fulfill the calling God had given them to go and preach the good news everywhere. In the process of doing this, they had mapped out a course for themselves. All was going quite well until they ran into a roadblock as they tried to go to Asia. Then they tried to go into a place called Bithynia, but again they were met with a roadblock. In both cases, Luke stated the roadblock was put in place by the Holy Spirit.

I would guess at this point they would naturally have asked the question, "Where do you want us to go?" At least, I hoped they had reached that point. The answer was soon forthcoming, as Paul received a vision in the night of someone from Macedonia begging them to come and help them there. Having received this clear direction from the Holy Spirit, they proceeded to make their way to Macedonia. Not surprisingly, there were no roadblocks along that path, and they were able to get to Macedonia and preach the good news there.

In my own life, I have seen God act in ways to direct my paths into His plans. In 2005, my heart was set on taking a mission trip. The church I was committed to, had several trips planned that year. The one I found most appealing was the trip to South Asia. One of the leaders of the church was going there to work with musicians to help them write and record their own original worship songs. He had already formed a relationship with them and had been working with them prior to this trip. He was also going to bring some recording equipment to them and help them get some things set up. Since I had a background in music and worship and had written my own original worship songs, I saw this trip as a good fit for me personally.

While my heart was set on going, there was a part of me unsure about it. I was at the lowest point of my life during that time. I was separated from my wife and going through a divorce. I felt like the least likely candidate that should be going on a mission trip. I was convinced there was no way at that time God would use me or want me to go. Yet I could not deny the strong desire to go. I would need some convincing that would put me into a place of certainty before I could wholly commit myself to the trip.

This convincing came in a couple of ways. First of all, the leader himself wanted me to go. He knew about my situation and still wanted me to come along. Also, I spoke to the senior leader of the church about it and was completely honest with him about where I was at in life. He spoke words to me I have never forgotten. He told me it was not about where I have been but where I was going that mattered. He gave me his full backing and support and encouraged me to pursue what was in my heart regarding the trip.

While this made me more certain than I was before, I still needed one final nudge. God didn't have to do that for me, but I must admit I am glad He did. I found out the best price for the roundtrip flight my traveling companion was able to find was just under $1,500. He gave me the details and encouraged me to get my VISA processed for the trip and book the flight.

Then, out of the blue, my boss gave me an unexpected bonus check for $1,000. The reason it was unexpected is the only bonuses we got at work were Christmas bonuses, and it wasn't Christmas yet. It was only October. As if this was not enough, the following week, he gave me another unexpected bonus check for $500. The message was not lost on me. God was paying for my flight, and by doing so, was giving me one final convincing proof, He wanted me to go. My boss knew I wanted to go on the trip, but he did not know the cost of the flight. The fact that the bonus money equaled the cost of the flight was a message from God I heard loud and clear to commit to the trip and go.

During this first trip to South Asia, God would speak to me, showing me I would return. He had more for me to do in South Asia. I would return 2 years later and have been to the same region a total of 5 times. Had God not seen fit to direct my paths into His plan for that first trip, none of the rest of it would have happened either. I am grateful He directed my paths and knew what He needed to do to convince me to go.

He Answers Prayers

Another way God speaks to us through His actions is by answering our prayers. It's one of the most basic facts found in the Scriptures that God answers prayers. In fact, it's one of the things that has always separated Him from the so-called "gods" of other nations and peoples. When we speak to Him and present our requests to Him, He truly hears us. The evidence of this is in the answers He brings in His way and in His time.

One of the stories of answered prayer that has always stood out to me the most was the story of Hannah, the prophet Samuel's mother. Here was this woman who, all she wanted in life was to be a mother. And yet the thing she most desired and longed for had eluded her. Being childless was a source of great heartache and sorrow for her, especially when her husband's other wife, who had given him children, would ridicule Hannah that she had given him none.

As the story goes, the family would go to the Tabernacle of the Lord in Shiloh once a year to offer sacrifices and worship the Lord. While there, Hannah poured out her heart to the Lord in prayer. As she did so, she cried, no longer able to contain the emotional pain and heartache that she felt. She asked God to give her a son and promised God she would give the son back to Him to be devoted to Him for his entire life.

While she was praying, the head priest there, Eli, noticed her and mistook her for being drunk. When he confronted her about it, she assured him she was not drunk and that she was merely praying and expressing her misery to the Lord in prayer. After hearing this, Eli told her to go home. Whether just to get her to leave or with sincerity, he told her everything would be okay, and that God would answer her prayers.

Having been encouraged by being able to pray so freely and by the priest's kind words, Hannah felt better and was able to eat something and go home with her family. Not long after returning home, her prayer was answered, as she became pregnant at last and gave birth to a son. She named him Samuel out of recognition to the Lord that she had asked the Lord for him, and the Lord heard her and answered her. When the appointed time came, true to her promise to God, she brought her young son to the priest, Eli, to be devoted to the Lord's service all the days of his life.

Little did anyone know at that time, God would raise him up to be a mighty prophet and leader of Israel. As if that was not enough, the Lord was kind and gracious to Hannah and blessed her with three more sons and two daughters. None of this would have happened without one woman's prayers and without God's answer to her prayers, which went above and beyond all she asked for and hoped. God took her simple, little prayers and answered them in big, amazing, and glorious ways.

Throughout my life, I have seen God answer many prayers. The truth is, one of the major reasons I follow Him is because I have seen Him answer my prayers. He does not always answer me in the way I want Him to, and He does work according to His own time schedule. Yet I have seen

Him act in response to my prayers, and I am convinced by this to continue seeking Him and pursuing Him.

Of the many answered prayers I have received through the years, let me retell one situation that stands out for me. A few years ago, my wife became ill very suddenly and was in intense pain. There was no amount of pain medicine to alleviate her pain. We took her into emergency, and a few hours later it was discovered she had a very large ovarian cyst that had twisted on the ovary and was causing unbearable pain. The doctors had no choice but to perform emergency surgery to take care of this.

The surgery was a success. They removed the cyst and had to remove the ovary in the process. Then, as if all of this was not enough, less than 6 months later, the same thing happened but to her only remaining ovary. Again, I had to take her in to have surgery done to rectify the situation. Thankfully, they were able to remove the cyst and save the ovary.

Neither my wife nor I were thrilled she'd had surgery for the same issue twice in one year. All indications were it could happen again and she would have to have surgery again when it did. The worst part was no one could really tell us why this was happening nor give us any assurance it would not happen again. Barring removing her other ovary, this could be a recurring problem for years to come.

Not more than three months after this, my wife began to have the same kinds of pain again, though not to the point where she felt like it was unbearable and required emergency surgery. There was yet another cyst, and while we could have scheduled surgery and had it taken care of, there also existed the possibility the cyst would shrink and dissolve on its own without the need for surgery. Ultimately it was my wife's decision, and she decided to wait and see what would happen.

Meanwhile, I began to pray with great earnestness. Enough was enough, and I was putting my foot down and saying, "No more." I was determined to pray for her until the situation was resolved without the need for surgery. It was more than just what I hoped for; I felt unwilling to accept anything less than that.

For the first few weeks, I prayed daily and persistently. Taking Jesus' advice to his disciples to be like the widow seeking justice, I was determined to pray and not give up until I received the answer I was looking for on my wife's behalf. Her pain level was not getting any better, but it was not getting any worse either.

Then, one morning, the Lord spoke to me about adding fasting to my prayers. He reminded me of Jesus' instruction to the disciples about prayer with fasting when confronting things not readily giving way to prayer alone. So, I began fasting once a week while continuing to pray daily and persistently for my wife's healing. I also made a point to lay hands on her and pray as often as I could.

Another few weeks went by, and things still were at a stalemate. She wasn't getting any better, but she wasn't getting any worse either. She had her good and bad days, her painful and less painful moments. The Lord then instructed me to add praying in the Spirit (praying in tongues not just with my understanding) to my prayers.

Weeks turned into months. We still saw no major improvement, nor did we see things get worse. Then one day, about 3 ½ months into this ordeal, my wife called me while I was at work. Her pain level had risen to a point where it began to feel unbearable. She thought she might need to go to the hospital. We both knew what that meant: they would likely take her in, run their tests, and recommend scheduling her for surgery.

That same morning, the Lord had spoken to me about fervent prayer from James chapter 5. I immediately recognized the situation was dire and the response was to pray fervently. I asked my wife to give it some time and to allow me to follow through on what the Lord showed me that morning.

I was in San Francisco at a job site at the time of her call, and the entire drive back to the office, I prayed with everything I had. I gave it my all and poured out my heart before the Lord with as much fervency as I could muster. I knew it was the Spirit enabling me, to be sure, and that it was no mere human effort on my part to pray with such force.

A few hours later, I spoke to my wife, and the pain had subsided once more to a manageable level. She determined she did not need to go to the hospital, and so we resumed our wait-and-see approach, hoping we would get an answer through prayer as we persisted in prayer, with fasting, in the Spirit, and with fervency.

It was at this time the Lord instructed me to add one final element: agreement. The Lord reminded me of the promise He made to His disciples "If two of you on earth agree about anything they ask for, it will be done for them by my Father in heaven" (Matthew 18:19). The Lord was telling me not just to pray FOR my wife, but to pray WITH my wife and to come into agreement together regarding her health and need for healing.

As I had done with the other instructions He had given me along the way, I took this last one to heart as well and began to agree in prayer with my wife for her healing. I didn't neglect the other elements but added this element to what I was already being led to do.

Then, about two weeks into May, my wife shared some news with me. She told me she had been pain-free for about two weeks! She waited to tell me to make sure it wasn't just a momentary respite but the pain was truly gone. Since she had not noticed any pain for the two-week period, she felt it safe to conclude she was healed and safer still to tell me about it.

Words cannot express the joy I felt at that moment. To reach this point, given all that had happened over that year – with two surgeries and nearly 5 months of constant pain and discomfort – my joy was unspeakable and inexpressible. I was so thrilled about my wife's good report, and I was profoundly grateful God had heard and answered our prayers in such a glorious way.

He Gives Good Gifts

The final way I want to highlight that God speaks to us through His actions is He gives us good gifts. We know from His Word the greatest gift God has given us is His Son, Jesus. Jesus was, is, and always will be God's best gift to us. By sending Jesus to us, God revealed Himself to us in a way that made who He is plain, evident, and real. Jesus rightfully declared to His disciples that in seeing Him they were seeing the Father. The invisible God was made known through God becoming man in the visible person of Jesus.

Furthermore, through Jesus, God gives us the highest and best gift – eternal life through Him who died for us and rose again. Eternal life, as Jesus stated in His prayer as recorded in John chapter 17, is simply this: that we know God, the only true God, and Jesus Christ, whom God sent into the world to us. This opportunity to have friendship with God, to be reunited and reconciled to God, and to have a relationship with God forevermore – this is God's greatest gift to mankind. It is a gift that never perishes, spoils, or fades. It is the gift we receive in this life and can take with us when we depart from this life into eternity.

In light of such an amazing and indescribable gift, the Scriptures also make known to us how God withholds no good gifts from us to meet our every need or to enrich and enhance our lives in every way. His good and perfect gifts touch the whole person, every aspect of our lives. He cares about our spiritual and physical needs. He cares about that which is eternal and temporary. He even cares about the desires of our hearts, and He knows best how to satisfy those desires with the good gifts He has prepared in advance for us.

So, what good gifts do we see God giving people throughout the Scriptures that highlight this aspect of how He speaks to us? I mentioned earlier God gave Hannah children and made her a mother. God also gave Abraham and Sarah a son, the child of promise. He showed Himself faithful and powerful, as Sarah had been barren previously and both Abraham and Sarah were old and past the usual age they would have expected to have children.

He gave Solomon wisdom to rule, and He did so in such a way as to make him the wisest man alive. He gave Bezalel and Oholiab knowledge and skill in making artistic designs and in various artistic crafts as well as the ability to teach these things to others – so that they could construct the Lord's tabernacle in every detail God had revealed to Moses. He gave David musical skills, and David employed those skills in writing songs of praise and worship and in equipping others to be worshippers and to lead God's people in worship.

He gave His people Israel a land of their own – a beautiful land with homes already built and a land that was productive and fruitful, so they had enough to eat and live on. He gave them the ability to make this land their own by winning victories in battle over the people of that land and driving them out so they could take possession and inhabit the land. Once settled in the land, He gave them peace on every side, so they were able to dwell in the land safely and securely.

On their journey from Egypt, through the wilderness, and into this promised land, God satisfied them with good things and sustained them for 40 years. He provided the manna from heaven, clean, drinkable water, etc. He also made it so their clothes and shoes didn't wear out during their 40-year sojourn. In every aspect and detail of their lives, He cared for them and showered them with good gifts.

In all of these things and more, God has shown us He is the source of all good and perfect gifts. We owe all we have and all we are to Him. He displays the kindness and goodness in His heart towards us, even when we don't recognize, acknowledge, or give thanks to Him for these things. In giving us good gifts, He makes His love for us tangible, concrete, and visible.

I want to share an example from my own life of God's good gifts to me and how He displayed His love for me in a way that was very tangible, concrete, and visible. Anyone who knows me knows I love the game of baseball. I fell in love with the game when I was 5 years old when my dad took me to my first Giants game at Candlestick Park. I've been extremely fortunate to live in Northern California, where two professional teams play less than an hour away from me. My opportunities to go to the ballpark have been many and varied through the years, and I've been able to make many fond memories over the years.

Many years ago, it was Father's Day weekend. It was Saturday morning, and I was getting my oil changed at my car mechanic's shop. I had my heart set on going to the Oakland A's game with my son, but I hadn't bought tickets yet and hadn't completely decided that was what we were going to do.

While waiting for my car to be finished, a friend of mine called me to see what I was doing for Father's Day. He had a daughter who he would be spending time with that weekend. He had gotten tickets to that day's game, but his daughter did not want to go. So, he was calling to ask me if I wanted the tickets and wanted to use them to take my son.

I accepted, and since he literally lived around the corner from my mechanic – I told him I would stop by to get the tickets after my oil change was completed. I was astonished by the timing of my thoughts about going to the game and my friend calling me to offer me tickets to the game! Not only that, but the seats were prime seats, as we were only a few rows from the field itself.

A few weeks later, I was planning some time off and some activities with my son for the 4th of July weekend. The A's had a game the night before the 4th of July and were planning a fireworks show after the game that night. I was talking to my aunt one night at dinner about my plans, and she mentioned that a friend of hers had season tickets and might not be using them for the night that I wanted to go. Not only did her friend have tickets but also a parking pass. So, she called her friend and found out she was not going to that game and was happy to give the tickets and parking pass to me to go to that game with my son!

Keep in mind I didn't ask for these tickets – they were offered to me. The tickets my aunt's friend had were in the 2nd deck but almost completely behind home plate. As I was picking up my son, I made an off-handed comment to the Lord. Jokingly, I said, are you ever going to let me pay for game tickets again? I assumed at some point I would have to pay for game tickets – but I was also curious to see how long this streak of good favor would last. Honestly, I figured this game would probably be the last one.

About a month later, I planned another game to go to with my son. I called my aunt to see if her friend's tickets were available for that game. Unfortunately, her friend was going to the game that night. No problem, it was worth a shot to ask.

I drove out to the stadium, and the realization began to hit me: I was going to have to buy tickets to this game. No big deal. Getting two free games in a row was amazing, and I was deeply grateful.

We parked, and we walked over to the ticket window so I could buy us the best possible seats. As I got to the window and began to ask about tickets, some people ran to the railing right above us and exclaimed they had two tickets they were not going to be using that night and were GIVING THEM TO US! Random, complete strangers showed up at the PERFECT moment with tickets.

I was speechless and astonished even more than the other two times. I was literally at the ticket window preparing to purchase tickets when that night's FREE game tickets were offered and handed to me. Somewhere, I knew God was smiling and laughing, getting a good kick out of this 3rd surprise blessing of free game tickets.

These seats were also amazing – just a few rows from the field. I was awestruck; I didn't know what to say anymore.

Such a silly thing – baseball tickets. Yet the Lord aligned it, so I got free tickets to 3 games IN A ROW.

There was a message in all of this. I had really been struggling with my own sense of worth and worthiness for a while, and the fact that God gifted me with baseball tickets showed me not just He loved me but He DELIGHTED in me. Here was my Father, getting a kick out of giving me GOOD GIFTS. Gifts that He KNEW I would love and appreciate and would be extra special to me as a lifelong baseball fan.

The biggest takeaway for me in all of this was if my Father was willing to bless me and shower me with good gifts such as baseball tickets, how much more did He love and care about me in the more important things in my life, in the things that REALLY MATTERED. The message He was sending me through these events hit home. If I needed convincing of His love for me and of my worth to Him, this got the message to me LOUD AND CLEAR. His love for me was unequivocal and unmistakable. This show of His love hit the mark in my heart and forever left a mark in me. His love for me was real, and He was delighted to show it to me, his dearly loved son.

Many years later, I would get free tickets to an A's game for Father's Day weekend from another friend of mine who desperately wanted to go and take his son but was not going to be able to go. Included with these tickets was the opportunity to play catch before the game ON THE FIELD ITSELF with my son! Other than the fact that it was unbearably hot that day, we had a fantastic time at the game that day. I was reminded again of my Father's love for me through this good gift He had given me. I was also delighted by His outpouring of love to me and for me. He gives good gifts to His children.

In doing so, He reveals to us, among other things, that He is a good and perfect Father who delights in His children.

God in All Our Circumstances

There are times when we find ourselves in circumstances where it's not entirely clear where God is or how He is working. In those times, it might seem as though He is silent and inactive, somewhere in the background watching but not involved. Yet there comes a point where His presence and activity become visible, and at those times, we realize He was there and working all along. We look back over the stretch of time when He seemed to be absent, and we see that this was far from true. He is God in all our circumstances, working behind the scenes in ways we cannot always perceive until He's ready to reveal the bigger picture to us.

As an illustration of this, I think of the story of Queen Esther, a young Jewish girl who rose from humble circumstances (she and her people were in captivity in a foreign land) to become queen. After she was made queen, her cousin, Mordecai, became aware of a plot to destroy and annihilate the Jews. He informed Esther of this plot and urged her to go speak to the king on behalf of her people in hopes of stopping this evil plot from going forward and her people from being destroyed.

In her hesitation, Mordecai pointed out to her perhaps she was chosen for her royal position "for such a time as this," meaning in her position, she was the one person who could implore the king and save herself and her people from destruction. She agreed to go to the king and try to persuade him to put a stop to this plan. Before she went to the king, she asked her people to fast and pray with her that he would receive her favorably. She understood that going before the king uninvited could cost her life, but she accepted the risk and went to him anyway.

Thankfully, Esther found favor with the king, and he issued an edict that essentially granted the Jews permission to fight back and defend themselves. The tables were turned, the Jewish people were spared. In the end, the one who influenced the king to issue an order for the destruction of the Jews was publicly hanged.

Looking at the story in its entirety, God emerges in all of the details, and His handiwork is woven into the entire story. Far from being absent, He was working behind the scenes, ensuring His people's survival. Since they were in captivity and probably feeling the sting of that situation, He gave them a clear reminder in those circumstances He was still with them, watching over them, and protecting them. He had not forgotten or utterly forsaken them. In spite of their present circumstances, He was very much alive, well, and involved in their lives. When they needed Him most, He was behind the scenes positioning people and things in such a way they were spared, saved, and would see Him in it all.

One thing I've come to realize is there is a consistent theme running through every circumstance of my life. The theme is simply this: God is using every circumstance of my life to show Himself and make Himself known to me. This idea has become so ingrained in me when new or unfamiliar experiences or circumstances arise in my life, I ask God, "How do you want to reveal yourself to me through these circumstances?" I turn my circumstances into a prayer: "God, show yourself to me through these circumstances. Help me to hear what you are saying to me and see what you are doing in my life or through my life."

Life is not without meaning or purpose. Our circumstances, too, are not without meaning or purpose. Things may not be clear at the moment but may become clear days, weeks, months, or even years removed from that moment. I've learned to trust God in the moments where I find myself scratching my head for lack of understanding of what He's doing and why. If He is truly working all things together for my good, then I can relax in those times when I feel like I'm in the dark. I relax because I know He is in control, and I can trust Him.

As a simple illustration, I remember being on a mission trip where I was teaching about hearing God's voice and worship. In the middle of one of the sessions, the Lord showed me how my years away from missions and ministry were not wasted years. They were years in which the Lord's purpose in my life was for me to know Him intimately and then out of that knowledge of Him, to go and to make Him known.

When that revelation hit me, I was able to see the brilliance of what God had been doing in my life all the time leading up to that moment. His supreme priority in our lives is we would know Him and out of that knowledge, we would make Him known. It's not the other way around. God desires people who don't merely know ABOUT Him; He wants friends who KNOW Him by experience, which comes from walking in a relationship with Him. Those are the ones He can truly use to make Himself known to others and spread the good news about who He is and His plans and purposes for all of humanity.

So, all the more, we need to look at our circumstances as important and meaningful. We need to watch patiently as the Lord works in them and reveals Himself to us in the midst of them, using them to speak to us, show Himself to us, and make Himself known. When the time is right, He will show us the bigger picture, and we can look back and see all the details of His handiwork that led up to that moment.

Now that we have taken the time to look at the various ways God uses to speak to us, let us turn our attention to what His message is and the forms His message takes when He speaks to us.

CHAPTER SEVEN

What Is God's Message To Us?

I detest JUNK MAIL.

Advertisements for things I don't want and don't need. No, I'm not concerned about hair loss. No, I'm not in the market for any miracle medicines. No, I don't care about big savings on your latest deals and offers. Just leave…me… alone.

In addition to this, we all know some of the junk mail we receive is a veiled attempt to install a virus and other malware on our computers or other devices. So all the more, I steer clear of anything filtered into my junk mailbox. The last thing you or I need is someone to steal our identity or gain access to our valuable data and/or personal information. No, my junk mail ends up in the trash folder and from there, I delete it permanently and never give it another thought. Life is too short to give my time or attention to junk mail messages.

However, there are those very rare instances where something ends up in the junk mail folder that is not junk at all. It could be that someone we know changed their email address and the filter didn't recognize them, so they ended up in the junk folder by mistake. When that happens, we can move their message out of the junk folder and into our regular inbox and instruct our email service provider that any messages from that person are not junk. We know this person and welcome their emails and attempts to send us messages.

Unfortunately, many in this world treat God's message as though it were junk. They have predetermined any message that comes from God is something they don't want or don't need. His message filters through as a junk message, which they ignore, avoid, and delete.

The truth is God's message is the most important message we could ever receive from the most important person we could ever know. His message is anything but junk. It would be a tragic mistake on our part to let His message end up in our junk folder. But what is His message to us? What was so important that He took the time and made the effort to communicate with us, even going so far as to become human like us in order to get His message to us? Let's take a look at what this all-important message is He has spoken and is still trying to speak to us today.

God's Everlasting Covenant

The single greatest message God has communicated is He wants to be in an everlasting covenant relationship with us. He is God, and He wants us to be His people. He is the bridegroom, and He wants us to be His bride. He is the Father, and He wants us to be His children. His everlasting covenant delineates how we enter into that covenant relationship as well as what He expects from us and what we can expect from Him in that relationship.

The Scriptures declare the terms and specifics of this covenant, and when God speaks concerning His covenant with us, He draws upon what He has revealed about it in the Scriptures. For example, through the Scriptures, we come to know Jesus' sacrificial death instituted this new covenant and made it effective from that point onward. All who come to Jesus in repentance and faith receive forgiveness for their sins and enter into the new life and covenant made possible by Him. In Hebrews chapter 9, Jesus is called the mediator of this new covenant between God and man. Full authority belongs to Jesus to grant eternal life to those who believe and enter in through Him.

Once we enter into this covenant with God, He unfolds the terms and specifics of this new covenant relationship. He commits Himself to be certain things and do certain things for us. One major aspect of this covenant is His promises to His people. The greatest of these promises is eternal and abundant life through Him. The moment we accept Christ as Lord and Savior, we begin to enjoy this abundant, eternal life, which will be fully realized when Jesus returns for His people and gathers them once and for all to Himself.

In the meantime, God has given us His Holy Spirit as a deposit to guarantee this future inheritance that will be ours one day (2 Corinthians 1:22 and 5:5; Ephesians 1:14). The Holy Spirit is the first installment, and He gives us a foretaste of what lies ahead for us beyond this life. In fulfilling His promises, God is upholding His part of His covenant relationship with us.

God also reveals the terms and specifics of our role in our relationship with Him, giving us both a new identity in Him and a new way to live our lives that is superior in every way to the old way of life we engaged in before we knew Him and entered into this covenant with Him. In keeping with all of this, God will instruct, guide, and empower us to keep our part of this covenant relationship with Him. It is the Holy Spirit He has given us and who lives in us who makes all of these resources available to help us and make it possible for us to live out this new life in Him.

The covenant is the supreme message God has spoken and by which He speaks to us. All of His communications relate back in some way to His covenant with us. The covenant is the whole message; the terms and specifics He declares are integrated parts of that whole. Let us take a deeper look at these terms and specifics of His covenant with us. As we do, we will see how they are connected to the whole and fit within this framework of God's covenant with us. We will also become more familiar with His all-important message.

The Promises of God

One key aspect of God's covenant with us is His promises to us. God has made many great and precious promises to us, and He is always working to keep every last one of them. In doing so, He shows He is true, faithful, and trustworthy. By proving His commitment time and time again, He also inspires us to be committed to Him. The promises He has made are a major part of His covenant He communicates so we know what we can expect from Him.

What are some of these great and precious promises God has made? He has promised to be with us always (Matthew 28:20). He has promised never to leave us or forsake us (Joshua 1:5; Hebrews 13:5). He promised to give us the Holy Spirit (Luke 24:49; Acts 1:4-5; John 14:15-18). He promises to answer prayer (Matthew 7:7; I John 5:14-15). He also promises to finish what He started in us, supply all of our needs, lead us into all truth, and so on.

One of the greatest promises He made and kept was His promise to save us from our sins. This He accomplished through Jesus, who came as promised and fulfilled the Father's plan to be our sacrifice for sin. God also promised to raise Jesus from the dead, and because He kept that promise, we have in Christ the hope of resurrection from the dead and life forevermore.

From Genesis to Revelation, there are an abundance of examples of God keeping His promises to His people. God promised Abraham a son through Sarah, and so Isaac was born at God's appointed time. God promised to deliver the Israelites out of Egypt and did so through a great many miraculous signs and through the leadership of Moses.

God also promised them a land of their own, and through Joshua's leadership and victories in battle (which God helped them to achieve), taking possession of that land became a reality. God promised to make Solomon king after David. God also promised David one of his heirs would sit on his throne forever, referring to Jesus.

The coming of Jesus as Messiah and Savior was a promise God made and kept. Jesus' promise of the Holy Spirit to His disciples was fulfilled first on the day of Pentecost and then among all those whom they preached to and who received and believed the good news. These are just a small handful of the promises God made and kept as recorded in the Scriptures.

What about us? Paul states it this way about all believers: "For no matter how many promises God has made, they are "Yes" in Christ. And so, through Him the "Amen" is spoken by us to the glory of God" (2 Corinthians 1:20). What a powerful declaration Paul is making here! All of God's promises are a "Yes" to us in Christ!

By entering into covenant relationship with God through Christ, we can check off "Yes" to all of the great promises made by God and contained in His covenant with us. We merely agree with God (say "AMEN") His promises are for us and He will be faithful and true to deliver on all of them as they relate to us.

So, when we hear God speak His promises to us, we hear wonderful things in our hearts and spirits and can joyfully expect to see those things fulfilled which God has said He will do. In Christ these things are guaranteed. God, through His Holy Spirit in us, will remind us of these promises and work to keep His promises.

I can testify from my own life God is indeed a promise keeper, as I've seen Him keep His promises to me throughout my years of knowing and walking with Him. One example of this is He has never stopped loving me and never withdrawn His love from me. I used to think His love for me was dependent on my performance. If I served Him well, He would be more pleased with me in those times and would love me more. I also believed the opposite – if I was failing Him miserably, He would not be pleased with me and would withhold His love from me in those times.

While I was struggling with this insecurity, the Lord would reassure me He did not love me more when I did well and less when I didn't do so well. His love for me was not dependent on my performance on any given day or at any given time. He loved me with perfect love.

I have put this to the test more times than I can count. Probably the biggest test of this promise was when I had left the ministry, and my marriage was falling apart. I felt like such a miserable failure. I had failed to do well with the things God had given and entrusted to me. I felt so far apart from God that my heart ached intensely, and I just wanted to die. Yet – it was in those dire moments He reaffirmed and demonstrated His love for me in ways I knew I had not earned or deserved.

Not only that, but He finally dealt with my fear and insecurity by showing me what my true worth and value were to Him. His steady persistence and consistency changed me and made me whole in areas where I was fractured and broken. Because He remained true to His promise, I now know nothing can separate me from His love. His love for me will endure forever!

The Teachings of God

As part of His covenant with us, God is our master teacher. When He speaks to us, He teaches us all kinds of things. He teaches us about Himself so we can know Him. He teaches us about ourselves and who we are in Him, for He knows us better than we even know ourselves. At times, He will teach us things about others so we can better know, understand, and relate to them. He teaches us about His creation. He teaches us His ways and will. He teaches us about His kingdom and how it operates. Teaching forms the basis for much of God's ongoing communication with us.

The Scriptures throughout highlight this important aspect of who God is and His dealings with us. Moses asked God to teach him His ways so he might know and continue to find favor with Him (Exodus 33:13). In Psalm 32, David records God's words to Him: "I will instruct you and teach you in the way you should go; I will counsel you with my loving eye on you" (Psalm 32:8). Most notably in the Old Testament, God gave His people the commandments and laws so they could know Him and follow in His ways (see

Deuteronomy 29:29, the context being the renewal of the covenant).

When we get to the New Testament and the coming of Jesus, we discover one major aspect of Jesus' ministry was teaching. He was called "Rabbi," or teacher, by many. He spent whole days teaching the large crowds gathered to hear Him. Then, when He went off with His disciples, He took them deeper into the teachings He had been giving to the crowds and revealed to them the meaning of the parables and lessons. Most importantly, His life was a model and example of everything He ever taught them. They learned by hearing Him, but also by watching Him in action and experiencing God through Him. He was the perfect embodiment of God's teachings to mankind so we could know Him.

Toward the end of His ministry and time on earth, He told His disciples He would be leaving them to return to the Father. He encouraged them by telling them when He did, He would send the Holy Spirit to them. The Holy Spirit would teach them all things and remind them of everything Jesus had said (John 14:26). Not only would He teach them, but He would also empower them to teach others. Before ascending into heaven, Jesus commissioned them to go to all nations and make disciples, teaching them to obey everything He had taught and commanded them.

In all of these instances, we see the importance of teaching to God. When He speaks to us, we can expect He will teach us too. His end goal in this is so we can know Him and be like Him, and from there He desires us to teach others and reproduce and replicate those teachings in others He's deposited into our lives.

Personally, I am thankful for all God has taught me over the years I have walked with Him. I've discovered He is a patient teacher who will repeat the things He has said and remind me of them regularly. Moreover, He will demonstrate in my life the things He's teaching me, which has served to strengthen and reinforce those teachings in my life. For all He has done for me and taught me, I try to apply those things in my relationships with those around me and pass on what I have learned from Him.

One thing He has taught me is how to be quick to listen and slow to speak. Through this, I have discovered most problems can be easily solved (or avoided) if I take the time to listen to what someone has to say before I respond to them. He has taught me to listen patiently, to get the whole message, and even ask questions to get clarification when needed. By developing in me the art of listening to others, He has also helped me to listen better to Him when He speaks to me. I'm thankful He has invested the time and effort to teach me this and help me understand its value in all of my interactions and relationships with others. Because it is an important aspect of His covenant with us, we can expect Him to teach us regularly when He speaks to us.

The Guidance of God

The Scriptures, among the many things they are, serve as a guidebook for us for this life. If we take the time to read, study, memorize, and follow the Scriptures – we will find them to be extremely helpful as we navigate our day-to-day lives. God did not merely give us the Scriptures, this guidebook, and leave us to figure things out from it on our own. Since He has invited us to be in a covenant relationship with Him, He has also committed Himself to be our daily guide through this life and help us understand His guidebook and follow it effectively.

The Scriptures illustrate for us how God has this role in our lives. In Psalm 25, David asks God, "Show me your ways, O LORD, teach me your paths; guide me in your truth and teach me…" (Psalm 25:4-5). David knew he needed God to guide Him, so He asked for God to do just that. In Isaiah 58:11, Isaiah makes this declaration: "The LORD will guide you always…" He wants very much to lead His people and guide them into His right ways and paths.

Jesus made it clear to His listeners He wanted them to follow Him. He declared about Himself in John chapter 14 He was "The way and the truth and the life. No one comes to the Father except through me" (John 14:6). In another place, Jesus called Himself the good shepherd and declared His sheep (followers) know His voice and follow after Him (see John 10:1-18). At one point, He made this incredible declaration and promise: "I am the Light of the World. Whoever follows me will never walk in darkness but will have the light of life" (John 8:12). Jesus came to lead and guide us from darkness to light, from death to life, from being far to being near the Father.

Jesus also promised when He returned to the Father, the Holy Spirit would be with us and also guide us. According to Jesus, the Holy Spirit would guide us into all truth because He is the Spirit of truth (John 16:13). In Romans, Paul declared that those who are led by the Spirit of God are sons of God (Romans 8:14). This again points not just to God guiding us but to guidance being a defining characteristic of what it means to be in relationship with Him. As a loving and caring Father, He guides His children into all truth and leads us in paths of righteousness and life. He shows us His good ways and enables us to walk in them. He will always lead us to Himself, as His greatest desire is for us to be with Him forever.

So, what are some examples of God guiding His people in the Scriptures? God led Noah to build an ark, showing him how to construct it – what materials to use, what size it needed to be, the layout of the space inside from top to bottom, and so on. As far as I know, this was the one and only boat Noah built in his lifetime, and it saved his life and family and all the creatures that came along with them for the boat ride. God led Abraham from his home to a land that would one day belong to his descendants. Abraham up and left his home and family and let God guide him to where He wanted to take him. God led Moses and the people of Israel out of Egypt and into the wilderness. God led Joshua and the people of Israel across the Jordan and into the promised land.

David constantly asked for God to guide Him, particularly as he went out to fight battles. David would inquire of the Lord before going to battle, and the Lord would give him directions and strategies which led to victories for David and Israel's armies. Solomon, at the beginning of his reign over Israel, asked God for wisdom to lead. God honored this request and gave such wisdom to Solomon that kings and queens from other countries traveled miles and miles to come and listen to all the wisdom of Solomon.

As a personal example, many years ago, one of my coworkers had been battling with some health issues, particularly some bad ulcers in his stomach. One day, the Holy Spirit told me to go upstairs to his office and ask him if I could pray for him. I was a little nervous about doing so, but I worked up the courage and went up to his office. I asked him if I could pray for him for healing for his ulcers, and to my surprise, he agreed to let me pray for him.

A few weeks later, he came and told me he had been feeling better since I prayed for him and his doctors had told him the ulcers had gotten smaller so they were able to do surgery on him. He was so happy and thankful for my prayers. I was greatly encouraged in all of this, as I had listened to and followed through on the Holy Spirit's guidance and now saw the good result that had come from doing so.

God wants to guide and lead us. He wants us to follow Him. He has good things in store for us and others when we listen to His voice and follow the guidance He gives. It also brings Him great pleasure when we listen and follow through on His leading. As we walk with Him in covenant relationship, we can expect Him to speak advice, counsel, wisdom, and correction as ways He guides us. He is our leader, our Shepherd, and our Father, and we have the opportunity each day to experience the joy and blessing of following His guidance in our lives.

The Commands of God

All of us love the promises of God. We treasure and cherish them. However, when we think in terms of God commanding us – issuing us orders or telling us what to do – the reaction or response is not always the same. In fact, it can be quite the opposite.

Why is this? Why do we love His promises but get turned off by the thought of God as our commander giving us commands and orders He expects us to obey and carry out? I truly think a big part of this is our fallen human nature, which wants to be ruler over our own lives and the choices and decisions we make. Yet those in Christ are new creations and have a renewed nature in Him. Where once we may have been ready to rebel against his commands, the new creation in Christ Jesus delights in God's commands and wants to carry them out. They are not a burden to us but a joy (see I John 5:3).

Another reason I think we are put off by the thought of God commanding us has to do with our misunderstanding of who God is. God is our Father, friend, savior, creator, promise keeper, and the source of all good things in our lives. He is also LORD. He is King of kings and Lord of lords. He is the one who rules all and sits enthroned. One day, as Paul stated, every knee will bow and every tongue will confess Jesus Christ is Lord to the glory of God the Father (Philippians 2:10, 11).

This is who He is, make no mistake about it. I love that He is my savior and He loved me enough to send Jesus to die for my sins, but He is also my Lord and King, and my life in Him — our lives in Him — are to be about following and obeying His commands since He is LORD. In fact, becoming a believer involves acknowledging He is Lord (Romans 10:9, 10). The bottom line is in this covenant relationship with Him, He is Lord and King, and we are to carry out His orders and commands.

Something else that's important to understand about His commands is the purpose or purposes behind His commands. One of the great purposes behind His commands is in following them, we will enjoy life and blessing as a result (see Deuteronomy 30:15-16). We follow His commands so good may result for us, our children, and for others who benefit from our obedience. That is a powerful incentive for obeying and keeping God's commands to us. He wants these things for us and for others.

Jesus also makes some powerful statements about the implications of keeping God's commands. In John chapter 14, Jesus says these words: "If you love Me, you will obey what I command" (John 14:15). The obedience we give to

God's commands is our way of showing Him we love HIM. In light of all He has given and done for us, the very least we can give Him in return is our lives and obedience.

Jesus goes even further than this. Look at these words to His disciples: "As the Father has loved me, so have I loved you. Now remain in my love. If you obey my commands, you will remain in my love, just as I have obeyed my Father's commands and remain in His love. I have told you this so my joy may be in you and your joy may be complete" (John 15:9-11). Here Jesus is saying by obeying His commands, we remain in His love and get to have His full and complete joy in us. How amazing! Given such incredible and lofty promises, how could our response be anything but complete, enthusiastic obedience to His commands?

So, what are His commands? What does God want us to follow and obey? Quite simply put, the two greatest commandments are, first and foremost, to love the Lord our God with everything we are and love our neighbor (meaning everyone) as ourselves. When asked what the greatest of the commands was, Jesus gave this as His answer (see Matthew 22:37-40). He even went so far as to say ALL of the Law and the Prophets hung on these two commands (verse 40). Love for God, as previously stated by Jesus, is to obey Him. Love for others is to love them in the same way God has loved us.

So, for example, just as He has forgiven our sins, we are to forgive the sins of others. Just as He has shown us kindness and mercy, we are to go and do the same. In every way, we are to be like Him in this world and to walk as He walked. Jesus' greatest desire and delight was to do His Father's will and obey His Father. If we are to imitate Him in every way, then this also needs to become our greatest desire and delight.

As we listen daily for His voice, we can expect there will be times when He will give us commands He wants us to obey and orders He wants us to carry out. It is one of the forms of communication He will use in His covenant relationship with us. The good news in this is He is working in us both to will and do His will (Philippians 2:13). He gives us His commands AND helps us carry them out, such is His goodness and kindness to us.

As a personal example, I remember my first full year in ministry in San Francisco. God called me into a desert season where His focus was exclusively on my relationship with Him. God wanted me all to Himself during that time. From a human perspective, it was a very lonely time, as a major aspect of this desert season was I did not have any friends and was led not to seek out friendships during that time. Here I had just left behind a community of friends in college and now entered this very isolated place where I felt cut off from human relationships and friendships. I struggled mightily with this at times, but since I knew He was calling me to this time and season with Him, I committed myself to make my relationship with Him my only friendship pursuit during that time.

By obeying His call and command to commit to this "desert time" with Him, God was able to lay the foundation of an intimate relationship with Him in my life. For the first time in my life, I was able to get up close and personal with Him and discover who He really was and what He really was like. What I gained in knowing Him was far greater than what I lost or gave up during that season. Not only that, but when this desert time finally concluded, God brought me the two close friends I would have during my time in San Francisco.

In His perfect plan and timing, He forged His and my relationship and then brought the friends I had longed for and He had planned for me when the time was right. He taught me the importance of obeying His commands and the good results that come when we commit to doing what He wants.

The Call of God

What is the call of God? When God calls someone, what does that mean? Is there only one kind of call or different kinds? Are calls general or specific, universal or individual? How does God's call fit into His covenant relationship with us? Let's look at these questions and see what answers God has given us to these questions in the Scriptures.

The most important call God makes to us is the call to repentance. Jesus told the Pharisees as much when they questioned him about why He ate and drank with tax collectors and "sinners." Here is his response: "It is not the healthy who need a doctor, but the sick. I have not come to call the righteous, but sinners to repentance" (Luke 5:31-32). The call to repentance is the ultimate call – the highest call – the universal call of God that goes out to all peoples of every nation, tribe, and tongue. God has made a way for us through Jesus to be reconciled to Himself. This is the good news, and it is the call Jesus said He had come to issue to mankind and He commissioned His followers to carry to the ends of the earth. This is the first and most important call of God, and in order to receive God's call to other things, we all must first and foremost respond to His call to repentance, to be reconciled, and to enter into covenant relationship with Him.

The Scriptures also give further definition to what this call entails. For example, in Galatians 5:13, Paul reminds the Galatians they were called to be free. We were called out of being slaves to sin and into freedom in Christ Jesus, by which we now serve God and others. In his second letter to Timothy, Paul writes how God has called us to a holy life (II Timothy 1:9). We are now set apart for God and to God, to live for Him. We are no longer to conform to this world's ways but to be transformed and renewed within so we can know God's will and good pleasure and live according to those things.

In his first letter, Peter tells his audience God has called them out of darkness and into His wonderful light (I Peter 2:9). When we lived in darkness, we did not know God or have fellowship with Him. We did not know His ways or follow them. Having come into His light, we now can know and follow Him and be His people, the people of God. These are some of the defining aspects of God's call to those who respond to His call to repentance. He calls us out of inferior things and into superior things.

God also has callings that are specific and individual to certain people. These callings may be to positions, roles, or assignments of different kinds. They may be long or short-term in nature. The Scriptures give us many great examples of this kind of call. For Joseph, he was called to rule and lead through a dream and saw the fulfillment of this 13 years later.

For Moses, God spoke to him at a burning bush and called him to lead the people of Israel out of Egypt. Joshua followed Moses in leadership and was called to lead the people into the Promised Land and lead the armies in victory over the people of the land. Samuel was called by God as a child to be a prophet to Israel. David was called and anointed to be king over Israel. The major prophets – Isaiah, Jeremiah, and Ezekiel – all received calls from God to prophesy to the people of Israel and the nations. These are just a handful of examples from the Old Testament of God's call on people's lives.

In the New Testament, Jesus called the twelve to be his disciples, follow Him, and receive special training and equipping from Him. Paul over and over states he was called by the Lord to be an apostle to the Gentiles. The church at Antioch heard God speak to them about sending Paul and Barnabas on their missionary journey, an assignment they had been given by God. Paul reminded Timothy about his calling to the ministry and the prophetic word through which he had received this call. Paul also lists the specific callings of apostles, prophets, evangelists, pastors, and teachers as roles ordained by God for equipping the saints of God.

In all of these examples as well, we can see the call of God goes out to specific individuals He has selected for a particular role in His kingdom work in the earth. Until that work is completed and Jesus returns again, He will continue to call people to these various roles and responsibilities as needed to fulfill His plans and purposes.

I can testify in my own life, I have experienced both types of calling from God. As a child, I heard God's call to receive Jesus into my life as Lord and Savior, and I responded to that call at a very young age. Then, in my early 20's, God called me to know Him and have an intimate relationship with Him, and that call has defined the last 25-plus years of my life in God. I have also received God's call to the ministry and a number of assignments through the years. – I've served as a youth pastor, worship leader, teacher, and short-term missionary, among other things.

Through the years, I've discovered my greatest ministry gift and calling is to teach and write. The material for this book I have taught on a number of times, and God called me to put all of this in book form, which is how this project came about. The call of God is a very real and ongoing thing in our lives, and we can expect when God speaks to us He will use callings at various times and in various ways to speak to us.

The Prophetic Words of God

When God speaks to us, sometimes the form that message will take is a prophetic word. But what exactly constitutes a prophetic word? Or, taking it a step further, what does it mean to be a prophet of God or a person operating in the gift of prophecy? Let's take a closer look at what the Scriptures show us about these things as we explore this aspect of covenant communication God uses with us.

A prophet is simply a spokesperson for God. God gives a message or messages to them for a specific person or group of people, and they deliver that message to the intended recipient or recipients. It's really as simple as that.

Both the Old and New Testaments tell us of prophets and their messages. In the Old Testament, God used prophets for a number of different reasons. Prophets could be consulted to hear from God when one of the kings needed direction, and so the prophet would go before God and get a word from God that helped guide the king and his people. If they followed the word from God given by the prophet, it would bring success and blessing. When they failed to follow the word from God given by the prophet, it usually resulted in disaster and death.

Prophets in the Old Testament were also watchmen. God would show them impending judgment coming on the people for their sin and unrighteousness and use the prophets to call the people to repentance. As it related specifically to the people of Israel, God would employ prophets to command the people to stop serving false gods and to return to Him, the one true God (Elijah, for example, in I Kings 18).

Prophets could also be employed to speak to individuals to bring about that person's repentance from sin. So, for instance, the prophet Nathan was sent to King David to confront him about his sin with Uriah and Bathsheba to bring him to repentance (2 Samuel 12:1-14). In these situations, God employed the prophets to remind the people they were in a covenant relationship with Him and call them back to their part in that covenant relationship.

Finally, the prophets of old were given messages that foretold of things to come. The greatest single message prophets of old were given concerned the coming of Jesus the Messiah. In declaring the coming of Jesus, the prophets were speaking words that brought comfort, encouragement, and hope. God would not always judge or punish. He had a plan to deal with our sin and unrighteousness once and for all. He had the means to destroy death. So, the prophets of old spoke of the ONE to come who would accomplish all of this and who would bring people of all nations into right relationship with God.

Many have wrongly assumed prophecy and prophets were used by God in the times leading up to the coming of Jesus, and when Jesus did finally come, prophets and prophecy ceased to be. This is a complete misinterpretation of Paul's words in I Corinthians 13:8-10. This stance also fails to consider what's written about prophets and prophecy in the whole of the New Testament itself.

In the book of Acts, there was a man named Agabus, who was mentioned twice in Acts as a prophet. He prophesied a severe famine was coming over the entire Roman world, which happened during the reign of Claudius (Acts 11:27-30). Later in Acts, he prophesied about Paul's impending arrest and imprisonment (Acts 21:10-15). In both of these instances, Agabus' prophetic words came to pass, which confirmed he was truly a prophet in the church.

In the New Testament, Paul lists prophets as one of the offices of ministry Christ has given to the church (see Ephesians 4:11-13). In addition to this, Paul also lists it as one of the gifts of the Holy Spirit in Romans 12 and 1 Corinthians 12. He states the purpose of this office and gift in the church is to encourage believers and build them up in their most holy faith. The end goal is we would be built up to the measure of the fullness of God. Since that still remains a goal to be accomplished in the church, then God will still call and use people as prophets or to operate in the gift of prophecy to accomplish His goals for us, His people.

Paul also states that prophecies are messages "in part" (1 Corinthians 13:9). What this means is that prophetic words are like pieces of a puzzle, not the whole puzzle itself. Each piece serves as a connecting point to other pieces, and so in this way, they play a valuable role for believers. For example, in I Timothy 4:14, Paul instructs Timothy not to neglect his gift, which was given to him through a prophetic message when the body of elders laid their hands on him. It's understood that Timothy's gift had to do with teaching and preaching, the ministry in which he was engaged from that time forward. The prophetic message provided him with a key piece in knowing God's plan for his life.

After receiving this gift, Timothy would need to get further instructions and details from the Lord about the where, the when, the who, and so on, as it concerned the use and employment of this gift. As Timothy acted on the part he was given and continued to seek the Lord about these other details, God would give him the additional parts he needed to keep moving forward and fulfill the calling he had received.

Finally, Paul instructs believers to weigh what is said (I Corinthians 14:29) and test everything, holding onto the good (I Thessalonians 5:19-22). Paul didn't want believers to simply believe and run with everything they heard. He wanted them to consider it carefully and hold only to what was good and useful. Part of this speaks to the fact that prophecy is "in part," so believers are to weigh the prophetic messages given and determine what part or parts the Holy Spirit wanted them to heed and keep from the word or words given.

Part of this also, though, is because Paul and the other apostles knew there would be false prophets and teachers among the communities of believers, and so they wanted to make sure believers were careful about who and what they were listening to and receiving. Thus, all believers, filled and enabled by the Holy Spirit, could discern the good from the evil and embrace one while rejecting the other.

In my own life personally, I have seen prophetic words in operation in my life and have been on both the giving and receiving end. On the giving end, the Holy Spirit gave me a word for one of my brothers about someone he would meet and encounter on a ministry trip he was headed on a few days from that time. When he came back from the trip, he excitedly related how he did, in fact, meet the person the prophetic word was referring to and made the connection with him just as God had foretold him through the prophetic word given.

For my own life personally, while I was on my first ministry trip to South Asia, it was prophesied over me I would return, as God had more work for me to do there. Within two years' time, an opportunity was presented to me to return, and during that trip, I made connections and a partnership that would enable me to carry out the work I was called and sent to do. From that first trip, four additional trips resulted in opportunities to do what God had called me there to do.

So prophetic words are one of the forms of covenant communication God will use when He speaks to us. They are still a valid means of communication He uses and employs today. We can expect through them God will instruct, guide, correct, encourage, and build us up. Because of the Holy Spirit living in us, we can be both the giver of these words and recipient of these words from others. God invites us to trust Him as to the who, the what, the when, and where this gift will be in operation in our lives. As long as our focus is on Him, listening to His voice, and staying true to His Word, we can be sure of His help, support, and guidance when it comes to prophecy and prophetic words.

The Pep Talks of God

As we walk in our covenant relationship with God, He knows we need many things to successfully navigate each day and the situations and challenges we will face. So, one form of communication He will employ is what I'm calling the "pep talk." Simply put, there are times when we need encouragement and when God will give us an encouraging word to inspire, motivate, and uplift us. He does this so that our faith will be strong as we live out the lives He has planned for us. He stirs us up to love and good works when He speaks His encouraging words.

The highest aims of pep talks are to help us finish the race, win the prize, and remind us of the hope of our salvation – that we will one day be resurrected with Christ. He will come again to take us to be with Him forever. So, for example, in Hebrews 12:1-2, we are encouraged to throw off anything that hinders or ensnares us and to run with perseverance the race marked out for us. As we do this, we are to keep our eyes on Jesus, who is the author and perfecter of our faith. We are also reminded of those who have gone before us and have already finished the race ahead of us, who stand as testimonies that if they can do it, so can we. They are now the spectators watching us and cheering us on to victory. Our faithful God wants us to finish our course and get to the prize. He provides encouragement so we will keep going to the end.

The other highest aim of pep talks – to remind us of the hope of our salvation – is also meant to strengthen our resolve and keep us focused on the right things. In I Thessalonians 4:13-18, Paul corrects the believers there in their wrong thinking about what happens to those who die in Christ. He reminds them when the Lord returns, the dead in Christ will be resurrected and gathered to Him as well as those in Christ who are still alive when He returns.

All of us together, then, will be taken away with Him to be with Him forever. In reminding them of the Lord's own words and of the hope of resurrection, Paul is encouraging the Thessalonian believers not to fear death nor to mourn the death of other believers in the same way the world mourns them. We have the hope of being reunited with them one day again, so this helps us in the present to stay the course ourselves with this hope rooted in us and serving as an anchor for our souls.

God, of course, is also concerned about the short-term and the day-to-day. In fact, He has given the gift of encouragement as one of the spiritual gifts to the church

(Romans 12:8). It is the responsibility of every believer to encourage one another and to do so daily (Hebrews 10:24-25 and 3:13). Doing this in combination with what the Holy Spirit provides can be just the boost any one of us needs. The Scriptures are also intended by God to be a source of encouragement for us (Romans 15:4). As we and the Holy Spirit draw upon God's good news and great promises in the Scriptures, we can be encouraged and overflow with encouragement to our brothers and sisters in Christ.

In the Old Testament, one of the greatest examples of God giving someone a pep talk is the beginning of the book of Joshua. Joshua has now taken over the leadership of the Israelites and is about to lead them into the promised land to displace the people living there and take possession of it. So, God gives a pep talk to Joshua, telling Joshua He will be with him, He will surely give them the land, and therefore to be strong and courageous. It seemed to work, as Joshua and the people of Israel, over the course of the next several years, accomplished all of this with God's help.

In the New Testament, consider God's encouraging word to Paul in Acts 23:11. Paul had been arrested and imprisoned in Jerusalem. People had been interviewing him to determine whether he'd done anything wrong or not. Meanwhile, Paul was eager to be free and continue to go to Gentile lands to preach the gospel. He had his heart set on going to Rome, as he had yet to get there though he had often longed to go. In verse 11, the Lord promised him He would see to it Paul made it to Rome and could fulfill his desire to preach the good news there also.

The rest of the story of the book of Acts details God fulfilling this promise to Paul, especially when dangers and perils and shipwrecks appear to threaten this from happening. Paul stood in faith in God's encouraging word and promise and in the end, he did finally make it to Rome and got to fulfill his desire to minister there.

In my own life, God has been a constant source of encouragement and pep talks. As much as I don't want to admit it, sometimes I get discouraged quite easily and this gets me off track. The Holy Spirit in those times always knows what to say and how to say it to me. In one instance, I had made some decisions about the direction I believed God was leading me in, and there were several people in my life at that time who criticized those decisions, even going so far as to question whether I had heard from God or not.

When the transition I was going through was over, the Lord brought many encouraging voices into my life to tell me I had made good decisions and He was pleased with me. It was the encouragement I needed at that time, and it gave me the boost that kept me moving forward in that season of my life. So be ready for God to give you pep talks as you need them too. He loves us so much. We are His great joy, and it pleases Him when we do well and succeed in Him.

The Revelations of God

When I say, "The revelations of God," what do I mean? Sometimes God will speak to us and give us knowledge or information we did not know before and could not have known ahead of time. He will also speak to us and reveal His secrets or mysteries to us, which are things we could not have come by through human reasoning, intellect, or effort. So, for example, when Jesus asked His disciples, "Who do YOU say that I am?" Peter responded by saying to Jesus, "You are the Christ, the Son of the Living God." Jesus then said to Peter and to all of the disciples present, "Blessed are you,

Simon son of Jonah, for this was not revealed to you by man, but by my Father in heaven" (Matthew 16:15-17, emphasis mine).

For anyone to know God, repent and receive forgiveness and salvation, and experience or encounter God, takes revelation from God. True, they must also act on that revelation, but revelation makes these things possible. If God did not choose to reveal Himself to us, we would not know Him; we would NEVER know Him nor enter into a covenant relationship with Him. Thankfully, He has chosen to make Himself known to us, and when He does this, this is divine revelation.

Paul understood this and told believers so in his letters. In I Corinthians 2:9-10, he wrote these words: "No eye has seen, no ear has heard, no mind has conceived what God has prepared for those who love Him, but God has revealed it to us by His Spirit" (emphasis mine). In the previous chapter to this one, he told them that "the message of the cross is foolishness to those who are perishing, but to us who are being saved it is the power of God" (I Corinthians 1:18). He further added, "Jews demand miraculous signs and Greeks look for wisdom, but we preach Christ crucified: a stumbling block to Jews and foolishness to Gentiles, but to those whom God has called, both Jews and Greeks, Christ the power of God and the wisdom of God" (I Corinthians 1:22-24).

What Paul is saying in all of this is that mankind cannot and does not understand or act on God's revealed truth; but through the grace and mercy of God, there are some who hear and respond to God's call and who accept this message, believe, and are saved. They come to know God through revelation.

As we begin this new life in Him, it is the ongoing revelation the Spirit gives us that enables us to grow in grace and in the knowledge of Him. What helped us to first believe is also what helps us daily. To the believers in Ephesus, Paul wrote these words: "I keep asking that the God of our Lord Jesus Christ, the glorious Father, may give you the Spirit of wisdom and revelation, so that you may know Him better" (Ephesians 1:17).

Revelation from God brings us to Him and into relationship with Him, and revelation through His Spirit in us brings us ongoing revelation of who He is so we can know Him better. In all of this, God uses revelation to make Himself known to us and bring us into a deeper relationship with Himself.

Paul expected that revelation knowledge would be a normal experience for the church. In I Corinthians 12:8, he lists the message of knowledge as one of the manifestations of the Spirit. In chapter 14, he instructs them about meeting etiquette when he says "Two or three prophets should speak, and the others should weigh carefully what is said. And if a revelation comes to someone who is sitting down, the first speaker should stop" (I Corinthians 14:29-30). What Paul assumed as normal for the church and what we should assume as normal for us too is God will be present when we gather together and will speak to us individually and will bring revelations for ourselves and for others, to encourage us and build our faith and knowledge of Him.

One illustration from Scripture of this gift in action is found in John chapter 4 in Jesus' encounter with the woman at the well. It's clear the two of them had never met and were complete strangers, but Jesus knew something about her he could have not known otherwise. He revealed to her she had had 5 husbands and the man she was now with was not her husband. Stunned by this revelation, the woman concluded Jesus was a prophet, because prophets heard from God and were privy to knowledge God would give to them. In the end, Jesus used this conversation and revelation to show Himself to this woman and lead her to believe in Him.

I have seen ongoing revelation in operation in my life over the course of my walk with God. This ongoing revelation is the reason that I know Him; it is not because I've studied, read the Scriptures, learned Greek or Hebrew, or listened to the most knowledgeable teachers and scholars on the Bible. I am certainly not saying those things don't have value, but it is possible to know a lot about God without truly knowing Him. The teachers of the law and the experts on the Scriptures didn't know or recognize Jesus when He came, though all of the Scriptures they knew and studied pointed to Jesus. The knowledge that comes from our study can only take us so far; revelation from God brings us all the way to Him.

Let me share a couple of examples of how God has used revelation in my own life. About a year ago, our church was going to have an all-day men's gathering on a Saturday. In the process of registering and paying, God told me to pay for two registrations – one for myself and someone else. I didn't know who the other person was, but I trusted what I heard from God.

I asked our pastor if there was someone who had not registered yet and might benefit from having their attendance paid for, and he immediately gave me a name. I ended up talking to this brother and confirmed he wasn't sure yet if he was going to be able to go. He had just started a new job and didn't know when he was getting paid and if he would have the money in time to register and join. I told him the Lord had told me to pay for two registrations and I was covering his for that day.

All he had to do was make sure he could go, and I assured him he didn't have to repay me. He was able to attend, and I was thrilled to be able to help him out. I simply received revelation from God and acted on it, and my brother was able to benefit from it.

One other quick example of revelation I have received dates back to when I was a pastor in San Francisco. I had been asked to preach at our Sunday night service, and I thought I was supposed to preach on Matthew 11:28-30, where Jesus invites people to come to Him and enter into His rest. I was talking to one of my friends, who also ministered in the church, and told him I wasn't sure what my message was going to be about for Sunday. I hadn't told him what I was thinking about or what passage I had in mind. He was going to leave, and then he stopped and turned around and told me he thought I should use Matthew 11:28-30 as my text for my message! He had no idea this was the one I was leaning towards, but in that moment, the Holy Spirit revealed something to him that confirmed to me I was on the right path. So that decided it for me, and I was thankful God had chosen to reveal this to me and confirm it through my friend.

Revelation knowledge is a form of communication that takes time to learn and get used to if you have not made it a practice before now. God is a great teacher and instructor. He is patient and willing to help us hear and learn His voice so we can walk in revelation from Him. He wants to give this to us so we can know Him and others can know Him through us. So, trust the Holy Spirit to lead you, and He will bring revelation knowledge into your life through your daily walk with Him.

The Warnings of God

Sometimes when God speaks to us, His purpose is to warn us. The ultimate warning God gives us is to turn from sin and the path of death and come to Jesus to receive forgiveness, right standing with Him, and eternal life. God also gives us other warnings too. He knows the road ahead of us and uses warnings at times because He loves us and is looking out for us. He wants to guide us away from temptation, the snares of the enemy, and the dangers associated with those things. As part of His covenant with us, He promises to protect us. So, He will use warnings as a means to alert us to danger and steer us away from it.

For example, Peter writes these words: "Be self-controlled and alert. Your enemy the devil prowls around like a roaring lion looking for someone to devour. Resist him, standing firm in the faith, because you know that your brothers throughout the world are undergoing the same kind of sufferings" (I Peter 5:8-9). Peter knew firsthand what the devil could do, for the devil had misled Peter to deny Jesus 3 times, just as the Lord had told Peter he would. Peter had learned firsthand what the devil was capable of, and though he failed in those moments, Jesus restored him.

Peter learned a valuable lesson at that time about the devil and his schemes. Peter had been caught unawares because He had ignored Jesus' warning to watch and pray prior to Jesus' arrest. All was not lost with Peter, and in writing these words, it is clear the lessons of his failure at that time were not lost on him either.

Jesus taught his disciples and followers to be watchful and faithful. In teaching them these things, He was warning them about getting lazy and shirking their duty and responsibility. He also warned them about the dangers of love for money, the dangerous influence of false teachers or prophets, the harmful influence of hypocrisy as practiced by the Pharisees and others, and so on. Jesus knew they would encounter many dangers in trying to follow Him faithfully, so He used warnings of various kinds to make them aware of those pitfalls so they could avoid them when they encountered them in their path.

In the model prayer, He taught His disciples to pray to God to lead them not into temptation but to deliver them from the evil one. His prayer for His disciples in John chapter 17 also included requests to guard and protect His own. Because of His great love for us, He warns us and prays for us and for our protection along life's road.

Paul, in his letter to the Corinthians, points out that the stories and examples in the Scriptures where people failed and it cost them dearly were written down as warnings for us (I Corinthians 10:11). So, we are warned by Israel's unbelief in the book of Numbers and the consequences unbelief had for them. We are warned by Peter's denial of Jesus after being so confident he would never do so. We are warned by David's falling into adultery and murder, that even a man after God's own heart can stumble and fall. We can look at what they did right and imitate that; we can also observe how and why they went wrong and learn from their mistakes and not repeat their mistakes and suffer the same consequences they did because of those mistakes.

God will direct our path through warnings. For example, the Magi in Matthew 2 received a warning through a dream not to return to Herod. Herod, as we know, had ulterior motives for finding Jesus. He wanted to kill Jesus. The idea of Jesus becoming a king meant Herod would lose the things he prized the most, namely his position and power. So, through warning them, the Lord protected Jesus from Herod's and the enemy's plan to kill Him.

God also gave dreams to Joseph, Jesus' father, which he also used to protect Jesus from Herod. In one instance, He led Joseph to take Mary and Jesus to live in Egypt to protect Jesus and to prevent Herod from finding Him. When Herod died and his son Archelaus became king in his place, Joseph was set on returning to Israel. Knowing there could also be danger with Herod's son as king, the Lord directed Joseph to take his young family to go live in the district of Galilee, in a town called Nazareth.

It's also interesting to note Matthew points out how this also fulfilled one of the prophecies concerning Jesus – namely, that He would be called a Nazarene. So, God accomplished much with His warnings to Joseph – He protected Jesus from those who would harm Him and He fulfilled prophecies written long ago about Jesus and specific details of His life.

I remember a time in my life when God issued me a warning that kept me from pursuing a dangerous and harmful path. I was in a dating relationship which was not a healthy one and was leading me down a path of compromise and poor choices. At one point, the Lord spoke to me I could continue in this relationship if I really wanted to, but it would cost me my intimacy with Him. Because I valued having an intimate relationship with Him above everything else, I realized if continuing in this relationship was going to cost me the thing I prized the most it wasn't worth it. Shortly after this, I heeded God's warning and ended the relationship completely.

After ending this relationship, God directed my path into some incredible learning opportunities in Him and a number of amazing ministry opportunities as well. I believe with all my heart if I had not let this unhealthy and harmful relationship go, I would have missed out on all God had planned for me at that time. I am thankful for His warning and its effectiveness. I am thankful He cared enough about me and our relationship to warn me away from something that was going to be a detriment to our relationship.

While it may not seem warnings are very pleasant things, they are useful and valuable to us. In our covenant relationship with God, He will speak to us with warnings when and as we need them. He is a good Father and a faithful guide who is always attempting to direct our paths in His right and good ways. He will always lead us into paths that result in our good, in us knowing His blessings, and in us walking in abundant life. So be prepared to receive His warnings when He gives them, and most of all, heed them for He gives them for our good.

The Conversations with God

I purposely saved this aspect of covenant communication God uses with us for last. Two-way conversation is the bedrock of any relationship, and it is also an essential element of our relationship with God and His relationship with us. God loves to dialogue with us, His people, His beloved children. The conversation was never intended to be one-way only between Him and us. He is not merely sitting up in heaven waiting for us to offer up our prayers and requests to Him with no response back from Him. He is not simply giving out instructions, commands, orders, guidance, and so on with no interaction from us involved. That is not a relationship. That is not the way He designed things to work with us.

It has always been His desire that communication between us would flow in two ways. He longs to engage us in conversations. Sometimes we choose what that's about; sometimes He chooses what that's about. In inviting us into a covenant relationship, He has invited us into this glorious interaction with Him.

All throughout the Scriptures, we see the people of God having conversations with God. Abraham, Moses, Joshua, Elijah, David, the prophets, the disciples, and the apostles all had conversations with God. In fact, Abraham and Moses are called God's friends, and I am convinced this is said of them because they engaged God in two-way conversations as a regular aspect of their relationship with Him. In Exodus 33:11, it says this about Moses: "The LORD would speak to Moses face to face, as a man speaks with His friend." Moses was not just a guy taking orders from God; He was God's friend. The two of them would have face-to-face conversations as part of that friendship between them.

One look at how Jesus interacted with His disciples shows us both the nature of the relationship He had with them and gives us a view into the nature of the relationship we also can have with Him. The disciples were constantly eating with Jesus, asking Him questions, engaging Him in discussions, listening to Him, and learning from Him. They enjoyed close fellowship with Him. He would take them aside and explain the parables He taught the crowds in greater depth. When the time came, He told them what lay ahead for Him – His betrayal, His arrest, His crucifixion, and death, but also His resurrection and return to the Father. He withheld nothing from them and was not detached from them in any way. He poured into them, invested in them, and He loved them dearly.

At one point, Jesus also called them His friends (see John 15:13-15). He told them they were no longer servants but they were His friends. They were His friends because they did what

He commanded them. They were also His friends because everything Jesus had received from the Father, He made known to them. They were no longer on the outside looking in; they had been brought into communion and close fellowship. They were not mere servants taking orders and rushing off to do what they were told. They were friends who shared life with Him and were given the understanding of who He was, what He came to do, and what they would be commissioned to do after He left. His mission became their mission. His work became their work. His enterprise became their enterprise. They were invited into partnership and friendship.

As it was with his disciples, so it is with us too. We are not merely servants. We are called to be God's friends. We are called into a love relationship, which is described to us as a Father with His children and a bridegroom with His bride; as friends having a face-to-face relationship and interactions with one another. All of these things point to close and intimate fellowship. Two-way conversations are the norm and the standard in our relationship with Him.

Jesus came to earth to be with us – He was called Immanuel, God with us, for this very reason. The high, glorious, lofty, exalted one also wants to be the one to walk with us in the cool of the day. This was His designed intention when He made mankind, and though we fell, His heart and His purpose for us never changed. Salvation is about being reconciled to God with the promised hope that we will be with the Lord forever – an unending, undying, unbroken fellowship. Those are the terms of the covenant He has made with us. This is the glorious invitation He has extended to us.

Through the years, I have had the joy of having many conversations with God about anything and everything. He is always listening, and when I'm done speaking, He answers and responds. I have shared my most private, innermost thoughts and feelings with Him, and because He loves me, He has done the same thing with me. He has loved me enough to make Himself known to me and reveal Himself to me. I can be honest and transparent with Him; I can be myself. I never have to be fake. It's okay to come and talk even on my worst days. He is there to listen and engage me. I don't have to be perfect. I don't always come happy, but because I've come to know Him, I always come knowing I will be welcome in His presence.

We have 24/7 access to Him always because of Jesus. We can come confidently and boldly, for we won't be turned away. Anytime for Him is a good time or opportunity for a chat. His door is always open, so you and I can freely enter and have a conversation.

These are the different aspects of covenant communication God uses when He speaks to us. All of them have their occasions and their importance. He uses all of them as He sees fit to speak to us and to engage us. Knowing them helps us to look for them and recognize them when He chooses to engage us in these various ways. In all of them, He is looking for us to listen to Him. In all of them, He is looking for a response from us. They form the fabric of our interactions in our relationship with Him.

Thus far, we have looked at hearing God's voice from God's side of the equation – why He speaks, how He speaks, what His message is to us, and the ways He communicates His message. Now we will look at hearing God's voice from our side of the equation. In doing so, we will explore the practical steps we can take daily to hear, recognize, and respond to His voice.

CHAPTER 8

How Can We Hear
God's Voice?

I am a musician. I sing and play two musical instruments – the piano and the guitar. I taught myself how to play the guitar in my early twenties. I had weekly lessons for piano from the time I was 8 until I was 13, at which point I took a year off. Later I had two more years of lessons from the time I was 14 until I was 16.

My first piano teacher tried very hard to teach me to sight-read music. However, sight-reading music was very hard for me to do. Sometimes I would ask her to play the song for me so I could hear how it sounded. Every time she did this, I would have the song all the way down or most of the way down by the following week. She caught on to this and stopped playing new songs for me because she wanted me to learn how to sight-read. I tried to do what she wanted, but unless I could get the sound of a song in my head, I would struggle through learning the songs she assigned me. It would take longer and longer for me to gain mastery over those songs. Eventually, I grew tired and frustrated with the way she taught me music, which was what led me to quit lessons with her after 5 years.

My second teacher exclusively worked with me on ear training. I remember times when he would start singing a song I wasn't familiar with, and he would want me to figure out what key the song was in and the chord progression and begin to play it on the spot. Due to my ear for music, I was able to figure out the song within moments and accompany him in whatever song he would sing.

Many people, including myself, have been gifted with an ear for music. I can listen to a song a few times, go find a piano or guitar, and figure the song out. In a very short time, I am playing it with ease. It is an easy thing for me to do. For others, this may not come so readily or naturally. They have to invest time training, practicing, and developing an ear for music to do the same things. Over time, it becomes easier for them to "pick a song up out of the air," meaning they can recognize what key a song is in, the melody, the chord progression, etc. Within a short time of listening to a song, they too can begin to play it with ease. They would be the first to tell you their training paid off and enabled them to achieve this level of proficiency in music.

What can be applied to your natural ear can also be applied to your spiritual ears. With time and effort, training and practice, you and I can learn how to hear God's voice daily and become proficient at recognizing His voice when He speaks.

So where do we begin to develop this proficiency in hearing God's voice? In sports, there is a term called an "A" game. This refers to a player or team bringing their best game – in terms of attitude, ability, and effort – to the game at hand against whatever opponent they are facing that day. However, before they can play their "A" game or perform at that level day in and day out, they have to put in the work to develop their "A" game. This involves dedication, discipline, practice, repetition, focus, etc.

In hearing God's voice, there are things we can do to develop our "A" game. In fact, the things we're going to look at in this chapter all start with the letter "A." If you and I will put these things into practice in our daily walk with God, we will develop our "A" game to the point we can bring our best into every day, every situation, and every opportunity to know and walk with God. So, let's begin our quest to develop our "A" game by looking at these simple yet important things we can do to aid us in accomplishing our goal.

The First "A": Awareness of God's Presence

In Genesis chapter 28, beginning with verse 10, we find the account of Jacob as he journeyed from his home to go live and work for his uncle Laban. He stopped for the night at a place called Luz and found a rock for a pillow and went to sleep. While he was sleeping, he had a dream in which he saw some steps that led from Earth to Heaven, and God's angels were ascending and descending these steps. Then he saw the LORD at the top of these steps, and when he saw the LORD, the LORD spoke to him.

The LORD told him he was his grandfather's and his father's God. He reminded Jacob of the promise made to them to give them the land where he was lying down, and He reiterated the promise of numerous descendants who would occupy the land and who would be a blessing to all the families of people on the earth. He concluded this message by promising to be with Jacob on his journey, take care of him, and bring him back to this land.

At this point, the dream ended, and Jacob awoke. It dawned on him at that moment the LORD was there in that place and he, Jacob, had not been aware of that fact – until now. Before God appeared to him in his dreams, this was just a place along the way as he journeyed to his uncle's house. Now, because God revealed Himself to Jacob there, the place became so much more. Jacob took the stone he had used as a pillow and set it up as a pillar and poured oil on it. He renamed the place Bethel – which means house of God. Having recognized and become aware of God's presence changed the place where he was staying the night from something ordinary into something special.

As he got ready to leave that place, he took God at His word and made a promise to God. He told God if He would truly be with him on his journey and watch over him and provide for him all the days he would be gone and then bring him safely back to his father Isaac's house, he in turn would make the LORD his God. He also promised that the place where he set up the rock as a pillar would forever be Bethel – the house of God – and whatever wealth God helped him to accumulate in his time away, he would give God a tenth of it.

With his newfound awareness of God's presence, Jacob continued his journey with confidence and assurance. God kept His promise and blessed Jacob all the years he was away from his father Isaac's house. He left his uncle Laban's house with two wives, several children, and much wealth. He returned safely to his father's house and even received a warm welcome from his brother Esau, whom he feared might still be angry with him over how Jacob had earlier deceived and cheated him out of his birthright and father's blessing. Even what he feared, God covered completely.

At the end of his journey, Jacob acknowledged God had held up his end of the deal they had made many years ago. Looking back, Jacob saw God had been with him all along and did everything He said he would do. At one point, Jacob even returned to Bethel and lived there for a time and continued to recognize it as a special place – the place where God first appeared to him and where he began to be aware of God's presence. He honored the Lord there.

He made every member of his household get rid of their foreign gods and purify themselves so they could go to Bethel and erect an altar to the LORD there and worship the LORD who had been so good and faithful. God appeared to him again and reiterated the earlier promises He had made, and Jacob in turn set up another stone pillar and poured oil on it, calling the place where the LORD had talked to him "Bethel."

The great thing about this account of Jacob is he became aware of God's presence at Bethel, and from that point on, he lived with an awareness God was with him everywhere he went and in everything and every way. Just like Jacob, this needs to be our starting point in how to hear God's voice. We need to be aware of His presence and know He is with us and very near to us.

For believers, God's Spirit lives inside of us – which means the house of God, or Bethel, is not just a place – WE are the house of God! He lives in us by His Spirit. The Apostle Paul said this very thing to the Corinthians when he told them their bodies were temples or homes for the Holy Spirit and He lives in us (I Corinthians 6:19).

Since this really is the case, then from this awareness should flow the understanding we can commune and communicate with God at any time, in any place, in any situation, anywhere. Since Jesus came to earth, the notion God is bound to a physical location – be it a city or a building – has been dispelled. He is everywhere present, and most importantly, He has come to live in us and be with us forever! With this in mind, we can view any situation as one in which we can hear His voice and any time as an opportunity for Him to speak to us!

This is not just a starting point – it is a glorious starting point! You and I don't have to wait until we attend a church service to hear from God! When we need Him most or just want to spend time with Him – we don't have to wait for a particular time or go to any particular place. He is in us and with us always, and this awareness becomes the launching point for an unbroken, unending fellowship with the King of kings and the Lord of the universe!

The Second "A": Attention to God

The next way to develop our "A" game is to make a practice of paying ATTENTION to God. Once we become aware of His presence and how He is with us everywhere and always, the next step is to make a practice of giving Him our attention, which gives Him the opportunity to speak and interact with us.

We see this most clearly illustrated in the story of Mary and Martha as relayed by Luke in his gospel (Luke 10:38-42). In this short account, Jesus had come to Bethany and paid a visit to the home of Mary, Martha, and Lazarus (though Lazarus is not specifically mentioned in this account). Acting according to what was customary in Jewish culture, Martha busied herself with food preparations for Jesus and the other guests present with Him. Mary, on the other hand, found a seat at Jesus' feet to listen to Him teach. Martha, realizing she was doing all this work by herself and not getting any help from Mary, insisted Jesus tell her sister to get up and help her! Jesus' response to Martha was that while she was preoccupied with all these seemingly important things, her sister Mary had chosen the one most important thing – to sit and listen to Jesus.

Because Mary had chosen the most important thing, to give Jesus her time and her undivided attention, she would not be forced to relinquish this opportunity to hear Him speak and teach. If anything, Jesus implied to Martha she should join her sister – not the other way around!

In our daily lives, many things and many voices vie for our attention and occupation. Inevitably, our lives are filled with many people and things. We might have school, work, time spent with family or friends, social media, and a host of other things we have or choose to do. With so many potential or actual demands on our time and attention, it becomes all the more important for us – if we really want to hear God's voice and know Him – to make giving Him our time and attention a priority. Jesus warned life would indeed have many cares and troubles. Even in the midst of all of that, He instructed His followers to "Seek first His kingdom and His righteousness," meaning put God first and foremost in our lives.

The sad reality is, people outside of a relationship with God live for their senses – for what they can see, hear, taste, touch, smell, and feel. The Scriptures declare as much, stating that people in the world have given themselves over to a life of sensuality (Ephesians 4:19). Life becomes nothing more than satisfying their temporal needs and desires. They live for what they can eat, drink, wear, etc. Life has become about earthbound, temporal pursuits and pleasures. Their ultimate life goals are about things that only pertain to this life and the realm they can see and experience physically. The spiritual aspect of who they are gets neglected to the point of numbness, callousness, and unresponsiveness – a total lack of interest in the things of God.

The unfortunate result of this over time is people dull their spiritual senses to the point they become hardened and unresponsive to God and the promptings of His Spirit or even the promptings of conscience. What used to prick their consciences or lead to a feeling of guilt or sorrow no longer has that effect. In this condition, darkness, ignorance of the things of God, and total separation from the life of God are the fruits of living life this way.

So, for us, if we are to know God and have an intimate relationship with Him, we cannot live this way. We have to abandon a life centered on sensuality and develop a life centered on SENSITIVITY. Hearing God's voice should be more than just a daily activity. It should be more than just a good habit. It should be a lifestyle and occupy a central place in our daily lives. It should be the highest of our goals in life.

The unseen, spiritual, eternal realm is greater than this visible, physical, temporal realm. Living for God and with God is greater than living for self. If this is so for you and me, then we need to recognize that to have the life that Jesus promised, we are going to have to give greater attention to Him than we do to all of the other things in our lives. We have to do as Paul instructed the Colossians to do- "Set your hearts on things above, where Christ is, seated at the right hand of God. Set your minds on things above, not on earthly things" (Colossians 3:1-2).

As we give God our time and attention, He will develop in us a sensitivity and familiarity to His voice, which is crucial in walking out the closeness and intimacy He wants us to have with Him and that is available to all willing to pursue it. The opposite effect over time will take place. We will be less given to our sensual cravings and desires and more driven and drawn to the things of God. Jesus promised if we would do this, all the other things would be given to us as well.

We no longer have to worry about or be overly preoccupied with the things of this world and how to obtain them for ourselves. God knows what we need and as a good, loving Father is willing and able to provide all of those things for us. If we set our hearts and attention on Him and put Him first above all other things, He will cover the rest so we can fully embrace, enjoy, and take hold of the life in Him that is truly life and worthy of our wholehearted pursuit.

The Example of Samuel

Before we move on, let's look at the biblical account of Samuel as an apt illustration of attention to God and sensitivity to His voice in contrast to ignoring His voice and the dullness and callousness that can result from it. Eli was the priest of the Lord, and as such, he should have made a practice of listening to and following God's voice and leading God's people to do the same. Instead, he gave himself over to the cravings of his flesh and taught his sons, who were also priests with him, to do the same. They even took it a step further, which earned a rebuke from their father; but by this point, they didn't listen to him, and he did nothing really to stop them or stand in their way. The three were altogether corrupt, living for their own desires and pleasures, dulled and insensitive to God and what God wanted from them.

Along comes the boy, Samuel, whose mom had promised to give him over to God. When he was old enough and the right time came, she did just that, and she entrusted her son to Eli's care. Perhaps if she had known the kind of man Eli was, she would have never done this. But as the story goes, she brought Samuel to Eli, and Samuel would learn from Eli to be a priest of God and serve the Lord.

Then it happened late one night when God showed up and spoke to Samuel (1 Samuel chapter 3). He called out Samuel's name. Samuel, who had never heard God's voice before, assumed Eli had called him and got up and went to Eli to find out what he wanted. The old man, so dull and out of tune with God, told the boy he didn't call to him and go back, lie down, and go to sleep. The same thing happened a second time with the same interaction between Eli and Samuel. Finally, on the 3rd time this happened, Eli finally got a clue that perhaps God was speaking to the boy, and he told Samuel if he heard the voice again, he should say, "Speak Lord, for your servant is listening."

Finally, when God did speak once again to Samuel, Samuel sat up and told the Lord to speak to Him. He received a message from God about Eli and his sons, which he later shared with Eli when asked about it. The message was they were going to die and would no longer serve as priests of the Lord, since they had made their "service" about serving themselves instead of about serving God and His people.

The message given by God to Samuel came to pass, and people recognized Samuel as a true prophet of God. From that point on, Samuel listened to and heard God's voice, and the things he heard proved to be true and proved to be from God. They showed God was indeed speaking and Samuel was really hearing from him.

This resulted in Samuel becoming a prophet of the Lord to the people of Israel and a leader and a judge of the people, deciding cases that the people brought to him to preside over and make rulings and decisions for them. Samuel continued to listen and hear God's voice. He made God's voice a priority in his role as prophet, leader, and judge of God's people.

The ultimate example of Samuel being attentive and sensitive to God's voice was when God sent him to the house of Jesse to anoint one of Jesse's sons to be king over Israel in place of Saul. Jesse, as it turned out, had seven sons. When Samuel saw the oldest, the first one brought before him, his first thought was surely this was the one he was supposed to anoint. He was the oldest and he looked like a fine specimen to be anointed king. Fortunately, because he had lived a life of attention and sensitivity to God's voice, God spoke to him at that moment and told him not to look at the outside and make this decision on what his physical eyes saw. For God, finding the right one was about seeing what was in the heart, not about what the physical eyes observed.

Having received this instruction, Samuel passed on the first son, then the next one until six of Jesse's sons had passed before him and all had been rejected. At the end of this, Samuel asked Jesse if these were all of his sons or if there were any others. Jesse told him there was but one left, the youngest. He was out in the fields tending the flocks. So, this youngest one, David, was brought in and presented to Samuel last of all. At that moment, God spoke to Samuel, letting him know David was the chosen one and to anoint him.

David would indeed become king of Israel and one of Israel's greatest kings of all time. More than that, through David's descendants, God would promise an heir who would sit on his throne and reign forever more. We know this is referring to Jesus, son of David. All of this came about because Samuel was willing to devote himself to paying attention and being sensitive to God's voice.

What was true for him is also true for us. Let us not follow Eli's example and give ourselves over to ignoring God's voice and living for sensual pleasures and desires, which leads to dullness and a callousness to God. Let us instead make our lives like Samuel's – one of listening, paying attention, and being sensitive to God's voice. The result will be a life that is effective, pleasing, and productive. Doing these things will enable us to hear and follow God and help us discover the paths that lead us into His good, pleasing, and perfect will.

The Third "A": Creating an Atmosphere

Once we have an awareness of God and His presence and decide we're going to pay attention to His voice, the next step is actually doing just that! To assist you and me in hearing God's voice, there are things we can do to create an atmosphere conducive to hearing from Him.

Life is busy and quite noisy at times. For many of us, it is also very fast-paced and frenzied. Something as crucial as hearing God's voice can be difficult in the midst of all of these things. So, what can we do to aid ourselves in the daily pursuit of hearing God?

One of the first things I began to do early on when I made a practice of hearing God's voice was to set a time and place to hear from God. In fact, given how busy my life was at that time, if I didn't schedule a time and place to do this daily, it likely would have never happened.

Jesus Himself did this very thing, so if we choose to do this, we can know we are in very good company. The writers of the gospels noted Jesus' practice when it came to prayer and spending time with the Father (Matthew 14:22-24 and Luke 6:12-16 for instance). Jesus would awaken before everyone else and find a quiet spot where He could be alone with the Father. After a long day of ministry, He would dismiss the crowds and even His disciples and go find a place where He could be alone and pray to His Father. He typically chose places that were secluded – mountain sides or gardens

– where He could have some privacy and quiet. For Jesus, these places were valuable and essential, and this practice made it possible for Him to have the time He needed and wanted for communion with His Father.

For me personally, I have discovered the early morning time works best. I get up before everyone else in my house is up and awake. It's generally much quieter, and I get to be alone with God. I find this extremely conducive to hearing God's voice and communing with Him. On any given morning, you'll find me in my living room with a cup of coffee and my Bible. I allow sufficient time – usually 30 minutes – to hear from God at the start of my day. For me, this has become a very useful atmosphere for listening to and hearing God speak.

Along with a set time and place, what you bring into the atmosphere is important. So, for me, I bring the Scriptures into my daily time for hearing God's voice. Whether you read the Scriptures or listen to them read to you on one of the many great Bible apps, becoming familiar with the Scriptures will enable you and me to hear from God more and better. Why? Because everything He speaks to us is either drawn from the Scriptures or agrees with the Scriptures. He regularly puts a Scripture in my heart or brings a Scripture to mind that becomes the basis for what He speaks to me. So, if I am familiar with His Word, I can easily find those Scriptures and dig deeper with Him into them and into what He wants to say to me through them.

The more familiar you and I are with His Word, the more opportunities we will create for ourselves to hear Him speak in and through them.

Sometimes I also find it helpful to have worship music going during my times spent listening to His voice. I have discovered worship also helps create an atmosphere conducive to His presence and hearing His voice. Even Elisha the prophet once called for a harpist to come and play before hearing a word from God (II Kings 3:14-16ff). Worship is the atmosphere of heaven, which is where God lives and dwells. Just read the book of Revelations and you can see worship is happening constantly in God's presence.

If that's the case, if that's the atmosphere He lives and dwells in, then let it be on earth as it is in heaven. Fill the atmosphere where you meet with God with worship and watch as His presence saturates that place. The result will be His voice can be heard more readily and easily.

Last but not least, bring the means to write things down. Whether you keep a personal diary or journal where you handwrite notes or thoughts or whether you use an electronic device to do the same, have something ready in the place where you hear God's voice to record or write things down as He speaks to you. This is also a wonderful help as it can be something you refer to again later in the day, or even weeks, months, or years later.

Many times, I draw so much out of going back and reviewing the things God has already spoken to me. They serve as great reminders to me of the things He has said and done, and they help me to remember those things. A lot of times, revisiting those things allows Him the opportunity to speak to you more about those things and take you deeper into understanding the things He has already spoken to you. So, choose and find what works best for you, but be assured having the means to write things down is another valuable way to set the atmosphere for listening to and hearing God's voice on a daily basis.

The Final "A": ASK Him to Speak to You

Once you set up the atmosphere for hearing God's voice, all that is left to do is ASK Him to speak to you and wait and listen. It really is that simple. Jesus told His disciples to "Ask and it will be given unto you; seek and you will find; knock and the door will be opened to you. For everyone who asks receives; he who seeks finds; and to him who knocks, the door will be opened" (Matthew 7:7-8, emphasis mine).

Hearing God's voice, like other things we want or need from God, begins with asking. If you and I want God to speak to us, all we have to do is ask Him. He promises us if we ask, we will receive what we have asked for from Him. He is the giver of every good and perfect gift, and He is a loving Father who delights to bestow good gifts on His children. With this in mind, we should be even more eager to ask and watch as He answers by speaking to us.

It's also important to note it's not just that we ask but how we ask that makes the difference. Here are some tips or aids to asking that enhance our asking and ensure we will get what we have asked for from God.

Ask Boldly and Confidently

The writer of Hebrews encourages us to "Approach the throne of grace with boldness and confidence so that we may receive mercy and find grace to help us in our time of need" (Hebrews 4:16). God does not want us to be shy about coming into His presence and asking Him for what we need. In fact, we are encouraged to come with boldness and confidence. We have been granted access through Jesus into the grace of God and into His presence, so we should take advantage of this and not shy away from approaching God. He welcomes us in with a smile and open arms.

John in his first epistle writes these words: "This is the confidence we have in approaching God – that if we ask anything according to His will, He hears us. And if we know that He hears us – whatever we ask – we know that we have what we asked of Him" (I John 5:14-15, emphasis mine).

When we draw near to God, we approach with boldness and confidence. Then we ask with boldness and confidence, knowing when we ask according to His will (for He is willing to speak to us), He hears us and grants us what we ask of Him.

Ask with Determination and Persistence

Jesus told His disciples a story of a persistent widow who continued to ask an unresponsive judge to give her justice in a legal matter that was of crucial importance to her. The judge tried to blow her off and ignore her, but because she refused to be ignored and was persistent in asking, the judge finally relented and granted her the justice she was seeking (see Luke 18:1-8).

I have learned over the course of the last 25 years when I ask God to speak to me, sometimes I have to keep on asking and persist until I get the answers I am looking for or need from Him. Why does God do this? Are there times He is listening and times He is not? I don't think that is the case at all. Many times, the answers to what we're asking for involve a lot of moving parts, so while it may appear God is not answering or responding to us, the reality may be that He was working behind the scenes and beyond our detection to bring about the answers we need. All the while, He asks us to be persistent in asking and not give up or give in until we see the answers manifest we seek. Sometimes that takes weeks, months, or even years. Even so, He asks us to seek Him UNTIL we find and knock UNTIL the door is opened.

There is an interesting account in the book of Daniel that relates to this very thing. In Daniel 10, Daniel described how he had received visions from God but not the understanding of the visions he had received. For twenty-one days, he fasted and prayed for God to give Him understanding, but none had come, and this troubled Daniel greatly.

Then, an angel appeared to him and gave him the understanding he was seeking but also explained what the delay was in getting the answers he was seeking. Here is what the angel told him:

"Do not be afraid Daniel. Since the first day that you set your mind to gain understanding and to humble yourself before your God, your words were heard, and I have come in response to them. But the prince of the Persian kingdom resisted me for twenty-one days. Then Michael, one of the chief princes, came to help me, because I was detained there with the king of Persia." (Daniel 10:12-13, emphasis mine)

What an eye-opening account! Notice what the angelic messenger said to him. From the FIRST day Daniel sought to get an understanding of the vision that troubled him, his words were heard, and someone was sent to bring him the understanding he was asking for. The messenger was delayed, having been detained on his way to Daniel, and with the assistance of another angel, he was able to break away and come to Daniel. Had Daniel given up at any point during those 21 days, he may not have gotten the answers or understanding he sought. Because he persisted until the answers came, he was able to get that understanding and an explanation of the things he had seen in his vision.

Paul describes for us what is going on in the unseen realm in Ephesians 6. He tells the Ephesian church our struggle is "Not against flesh and blood, but against the rulers, against the authorities, against the powers of this dark world and against the spiritual forces of evil in the heavenly realms" (Ephesians 6:12).

With this in mind, we have to know going into an endeavor to know God and hear His voice, we will encounter the opposition mentioned here in our quest. It's inevitable, and I believe it's one of the main reasons why we are encouraged and urged to persist and persevere and not GIVE UP. Let Daniel and others like him be an example to us of those who persisted and got the answers they sought and heard from God in spite of the opposition trying to keep that from happening. Their DETERMINATION needs to be OUR DETERMINATION – let nothing stop us from hearing God and knowing His voice!

Ask With Expectation and Faith

The writer of Hebrews has some instructive words for us: "And without faith, it is impossible to please God, because anyone who comes to Him must believe that He exists and He rewards those who earnestly seek Him" (Hebrews 11:6, emphasis mine). Herein lies one of the great keys to hearing and knowing God: approach Him with faith – that He exists – and He REWARDS those who seek Him.

If you and I are looking for something we don't believe we will ever find, then why waste the effort on the pursuit? If we begin our pursuit with the belief we can and will find what we're looking for, then when we do find it, we have the reward of getting what we searched for and the satisfaction of knowing the time and energy we put into the search was WORTH it. It's the same with pursuing God. If we start with the knowledge our search will lead to us finding Him, then when we do find Him and lay hold of Him, great will be our satisfaction in those moments as He rewards us with Himself in response to our search for Him.

In the case of what the writer of Hebrews was saying, the reward is promised to us by God. This is the same God who only speaks what is true and does not lie. He promises our search for Him will not be in vain. So, from the outset, with this promise in mind, we can seek for Him with the faith He wants to be found and is waiting to be found by those who will take action and seek Him.

There is a familiar saying, "Seeing is believing." But in the case of knowing God and hearing His voice, it's the opposite – believing is seeing. Or, in terms of hearing His voice, believing is hearing. Whatever way you or I phrase it, we must begin our quest to know God and hear His voice with faith. Starting with faith will lead to a positive outcome each and every time; because the God who we are searching for promises us it will be so and makes it so. He REWARDS those who, in faith, seek Him out to find Him.

Similar to faith, we must seek to know and hear God's voice with EXPECTATION. Expectation adds to faith an assurance we will receive what we are hoping for in the asking. It's much like my children on their birthdays. My children get more and more excited as their birthdays draw near, for they expect to receive gifts for their birthdays. They are full of anticipation and eagerness for the day itself to arrive. In their minds, when the day finally arrives, they expect to get gifts with their names on them. They believe they will receive, and so they are filled with hope. It's much more than hope to them. It's more than an "if" for them; it's a "when" for them.

This means when the appointed time and day comes, they WILL get what they have been waiting and hoping for, with no doubt at all in their minds.

It must be the same with us and seeking God. We must come to Him with childlike expectation that WHEN we come, He will be there waiting for us, gifts and rewards in hand. We approach Him with excitement and anticipation of good things from our GOOD, GOOD Father. We can't wait until the next opportunity to spend time with Him and listen to His voice. We are filled with wonder about what He will say this time around and what good things He has in store for us in our time together with Him. We look forward with joy to being in His presence and being with Him. This is how it should be, and it is how He wants it to be for us.

So, ask God to speak to you. Don't be afraid; ask with boldness and confidence since we have been granted access to Him and He bids us to come. Ask with determination that you won't stop until you get what you're seeking, for persistent determination will lead to the desired outcome. Ask with expectation and with faith – He PROMISES to reward those who seek Him and He is waiting for us with eager expectation that we will seek Him so He can be found by us. He wants to be found. He wants to be sought. He wants to be known by us. He wants to speak to us. So, make the effort to ask and add these things to your asking. He waits with excitement, His gifts and rewards in hand, for those who will seek after Him in order to find HIM.

As we move on from here, the next question that needs to be answered in our journey of hearing God's voice is this: when we hear Him, how can we be assured it is really Him speaking to us? This is a very crucial question that needs to be explored so we can recognize His voice and reject any voice trying to sound like His but is not His voice.

CHAPTER 9

How Can We Recognize God's Voice?

Sheep are not the smartest of animals. Without proper supervision and care, they will eat too much. This can result in a condition called, "bloat," which in mild cases will make a sheep feel uncomfortable due to the buildup of gas in their stomachs. In extreme cases, it could lead to death. Sheep are also prone to wander. They might do this for a number of reasons, the most common being to escape danger, to check something out they find interesting, or to stay with the rest of the flock. It's not uncommon for one to get lost or separated from the rest of the flock, exposing them to even more danger if they are isolated and alone.

However, there is one thing sheep can be trained to do well: to know and follow the voice of their shepherd. A good shepherd walks in front of the flock and uses his voice to lead and guide them. The shepherd will use distinct calls to get them to stop, move forward, or turn in one direction or another. Over time, the sheep will become familiar with and recognize the voice of their shepherd.

Having gained their trust and built up this familiarity, the shepherd is able to lead them and take care of them properly.

A random stranger's voice would not have the same effect on them; in fact, it might have quite the opposite effect. Having learned who their shepherd is, the sheep will listen to and follow the voice of the one they recognize while ignoring all other voices. In John 10, Jesus affirmed this reality in a story of a shepherd and his sheep.

> *"The one who enters (the sheep pen) by the gate is the shepherd of the sheep. The gatekeeper opens the gate for him, and the sheep listen to his voice. He calls his own sheep by name and leads them out. When he has brought out all his own, he goes on ahead of them, and his sheep follow him because they know his voice. But they will never follow a stranger; in fact, they will run away from him because they do not recognize a stranger's voice" (John 10:2-5, emphasis mine).*

This story contains the key idea we will explore in this chapter. In order to hear God's voice and follow Him and Him alone, we need to be able to distinguish His voice from other voices pretending to be Him. We must learn to recognize His voice while drowning out the voices of strangers and imitators. His voice, like a shepherd's voice to his own sheep, is distinctive, and we can and need to become intimately familiar with it. So, what is it about God's voice that sets it apart from all other voices?

There are certain distinctives of God's voice that ring true in all circumstances. Knowing what these are will keep us safe and keep us from following strangers and pretenders. The enemy of our souls will do anything he can to deceive and mislead us. So, it is crucial for us to know what these characteristics and safeguards are God has given us and expects us to use in order to recognize His voice and distinguish it from the many possible voices we can listen to or hear. As we learn and apply these characteristics and safeguards to hearing God's voice, we will become intimately familiar with His voice so we can hear and follow Him. It will become easier to recognize and reject the strangers and pretenders trying to imitate Him and lead us astray.

The First Distinctive of God's Voice: *Everything God Says Agrees 100% With The Bible.*

It is my opinion of all the distinctive aspects of God's voice we will cover in this chapter, this stands out as the most important one. It's also why I chose to make it the first one. God will NEVER speak anything that goes contrary to His words in the Scriptures. It just won't happen. Not now, not ever. If anyone claims to have a new truth or revelation, and that new truth or revelation does not line up with the Scriptures, then no matter how good it sounds to our ears, it must be rejected out of hand as NOT originating with Him.

Even Jesus, when describing to His listeners who He was and why He came, said these words: "Do not think that I have come to abolish the Law or the Prophets; I have not come to abolish them but to fulfill them. I tell you the truth, until heaven and earth disappear, not the smallest letter, not the least stroke of a pen, will by any means disappear from the Law until everything is accomplished" (Matthew 5:17-18).

What was Jesus saying here? These words are packed and loaded with meaning. First of all, think for a moment about Jesus' teaching. Some people thought He was teaching new things or, worse yet, He was teaching things contrary to what they already knew and learned. In actual fact, He was giving them the right understanding of the things already revealed in the Scriptures and correcting all of their faulty thinking and misinterpretations of the things revealed.

So, whether Jesus was teaching about the Sabbath, prayer, fasting, the commandments – you name it – His teachings were not intended to negate the Scriptures but to illuminate and clarify them so the people understood them properly. And who better to help them understand the Word than the One who was the Word? His person and life embodied and exemplified everything the words of Scripture said and meant.

This leads me to my next point. Not only did He teach a correct understanding of the revelation they had in the Scriptures – He lived it out in every way. He embodied the Word and modeled for them what it truly meant to fulfill the things written in them and live them out fully, completely, and correctly. Jesus, for example, demonstrated the proper way to live on the Sabbath. He helped those in need and healed those who were hurting and broken on the Sabbath. Some accused Him, in doing this, of violating the rule about the Sabbath of not doing any work. Jesus, however, pointed them to the reality about the Sabbath – that doing good on the Sabbath was not forbidden and to forego doing good on the Sabbath was actually a greater violation of the Law than if He had actually done work on the Sabbath. In this way, He attempted to show them the true meaning and understanding of the Sabbath and of the Law – to do good, to show mercy, to love one's neighbor.

Inasmuch as Jesus fulfilled the Law in everything He said and did, He showed He agreed and was in alignment with what had been revealed in the Scriptures. Even more than this, He had also come as the fulfillment of the things written about Him in the Scriptures – the promises God had made through them long ago. These were the prophetic words and declarations that spoke of Him centuries before His appearance on earth.

Matthew, in His gospel, made a point to connect the two things – the prophetic declarations made in times past with their fulfillment in the person, work, and life of Jesus. Jesus came to be the fulfillment of all those things and, in doing so, showed He was truly sent from the Father and was the Son of God incarnate in human flesh.

What does all of this have to do with hearing God's voice? Simply this: had Jesus been a pretender or impersonator, His words, teachings, works, and life would not have been so fully and completely aligned with the Scriptures. But the reality is, everything about Him embodied them, exemplified them, and showed us what it looks like to be in perfect agreement and alignment with the Scriptures. If this had not been so, then it would have been right and proper for the people of Jesus' time to reject Him as the one sent from God and conclude He was not the Messiah they had been waiting for all of this time.

Consider also when He was in the wilderness being tempted by the devil, the devil misquoted Scripture to Jesus in an attempt to get Jesus to sin and violate God's Word. Jesus' response was to quote Scripture back to the devil, but correctly and accurately. Again, Jesus showed His complete agreement and alignment with the Scriptures; He did not come to violate the Scriptures or live independently of them but to submit Himself fully and completely to all that was written in them.

It's also helpful for us to look at how the disciples and the early church in the book of Acts used the Scriptures to interpret and understand the things they were hearing or experiencing as a test to see if those things were from God or not. From the very first day the church was born on the day of Pentecost, the Scriptures were key to understanding and making sense of what was happening and determining if it was God or not.

While some onlookers judged those who were speaking in tongues were probably drunk with too much wine, the Holy Spirit helped Peter to connect what was happening at that moment to a prophetic promise that had been made by the prophet Joel many centuries ago. In doing this, Peter showed those present what the disciples were experiencing, and the eyewitnesses were observing, was a fulfillment of the Scriptures and in agreement with the Scriptures. Therefore, Peter concluded what was happening was from God, and he was able to use the opportunity presented by this outpouring of the Spirit to preach the good news and lead 3,000 people to become believers in Jesus that day.

Later on, in the book of Acts, we see the gospel was preached and proclaimed to Gentiles, and they too became believers. God poured out His Spirit on those Gentile believers and they also spoke in other languages and experienced the same things as the disciples did on the day of Pentecost. Paul observed that signs, wonders, and miracles took place in his ministry among the Gentiles, which showed God was moving among the Gentiles in the same way He was moving among the Jews. All of this was evidence God was accepting the Gentiles and bringing them into His kingdom and into the community of believers.

The Scriptures also confirmed this to them, providing them evidence God had a plan for the Gentiles to include them in both the outpouring of His Spirit and salvation for all humanity. Since both the Scriptures and what was happening among the Gentiles agreed with one another, this enabled the Jewish leaders of the early church to both accept and welcome the Gentiles as fellow believers in Christ and accept their faith in Christ as just as valid as their own faith in Him.

This meant the church would not end up merely being a local Jewish sect but would become what God intended it to be – a worldwide community comprised of all peoples, nations, tribes, and tongues – all of whom were meant to hear the gospel of Jesus and be given an opportunity to believe and receive God's free gift of eternal life through His Son.

One final example from Acts, of the early believers using the Scriptures as a measuring line to confirm if something was from God or not, was the practice of the believers at Berea. In Acts 17, verse 11, Luke says this about those in Berea: "Now the Bereans were of more noble character than the Thessalonians, for they received the message (the gospel Paul preached to them) with great eagerness and examined the Scriptures every day to see if what Paul said was true" (emphasis mine).

Their approach needs to be our approach to hearing from God – eagerness and examination. They were happy to hear the good news Paul preached (their eagerness), but they were also careful to check and confirm if what he was saying was really true and aligned with what the Scriptures had revealed (their examination). Having searched the

Scriptures and having confirmed what Paul was preaching was in fact in agreement with what had been revealed in the Scriptures, many Bereans then believed Paul's message and became followers of Jesus. In doing this, they gave us a template for how to hear God and how to confirm if it is really Him speaking to us. They engaged Paul's message with the understanding if it was from God, it would agree 100% with the Scriptures.

Let me share a personal example of how I used the Scriptures to confirm what I believed to be God's voice speaking to me. I was in college studying to go into ministry, for I believed God had called me to be in ministry. Since the time I was fourteen years old, I believed God's plan for my life was for me to become a missionary to the nations. I accepted this call without doubt or question. But sometime around my senior year of college, I was starting to have some doubts and to feel unsure about this call.

I was taking a walk with a friend and talking about this. I remember asking my friend if he thought God had really called me to go into the ministry or not or if I had been wrong about it. His words were the perfect answer I needed. He said he wasn't sure if I had heard from God or not, but he was definitely sure I hadn't heard from the devil – as the last thing the devil would tell me to do would be to go into the world, preach the good news, and make disciples!

When my friend said this, it enabled me to look at my calling from God from an angle I had not considered before up until that point. By ruling out the devil as the source of my call – because never in a million years would the devil tell anyone to go and preach Jesus to the world – it helped me to embrace the fact only God would have placed such a call on my life.

The Scriptures confirmed what I believed I had heard from God many years previously. The last words of Jesus to His disciples before leaving earth and returning to the Father were a command for them to go into all the world, preach the good news, and make disciples (see Matthew 28:19-20). At the very least, I concluded, in following what I believed was God's calling on my life, I was acting in agreement with the Scriptures. I was living out something I knew God had said in His Word.

Knowing this, I felt it was reasonable to believe I had heard from God and to continue my pursuit of following the calling He had given me. Because my calling agreed with His words in the Scriptures, my doubts gave way to certainty once more.

The Second Distinctive of God's Voice: *God Always Speaks the Truth*

God always tells the truth. He never lies. In fact, the Scriptures declare He does not lie. The prophet Balaam, in one of his prophetic utterances in the book of Numbers, says these words: "God is not a man, that He should lie, nor a son of man, that He should change His mind. Does He speak and then not act? Does He promise and not fulfill?" (Numbers 23:19).

When God speaks, He is utterly and completely consistent in all that He says. What He speaks is consistent with His nature and His character; what He speaks is consistent with His actions and works. He does not contradict Himself in any way. He is trustworthy, and, therefore, His words are also trustworthy.

In the New Testament, Paul stated in his introductory words in his letter to Titus how the hope of eternal life was a promise God made before the beginning of time and then at the appointed season, He brought this to light through the preaching of the gospel. In saying all this, Paul said to Titus this promise hinged on the fact God does not lie. John, in the first of his three epistles, declared God is light and there is no darkness at all in Him. James, in his epistle, stated God does not change like shifting shadows. All of this is to say God speaks the truth, acts consistent with the truth of what He speaks, and is Himself the Truth (see Jesus' assertion to this in John 14:6).

If you and I consider the whole of Scripture, both the Old and New Testaments, the two parts complement one another in that the Old is where the great promise of the coming of Jesus to save us is stated and the New is where we see this come to pass just as God promised it would.

It is why they celebrated the birth of Jesus with such great joy; here at last had come the long-awaited one, the one God had promised centuries before to send to earth. And now that promise was being fulfilled in the birth and coming of Jesus, thus proving God was true to His Word and His promises made in it.

Not only was His birth and coming a fulfillment of a promise – His death on our behalf was also the fulfillment of a promise. God promised to make a way for us to be forgiven. God promised His Son would come and die for us so we could receive forgiveness and have new life. Jesus, by going to the cross and finishing the work He was sent to do, also fulfilled God's promise by being the sacrifice for sin and instituting the new covenant by which we can become clean and acceptable in God's sight once and for all. All of this shows God is true to His words and acts completely to fulfill His words and promises.

Think about the story of the Garden of Eden, where Adam and Eve were tempted and deceived by the serpent, the devil. Essentially, the devil asserted to them God lied to them when he told them if they ate the fruit from the forbidden tree they would die. He contradicted what God told them in an effort (that sadly succeeded) to get them to disobey God but also to get them not to trust God or His Words.

The devil has been doing that ever since. Jesus, when speaking about the devil in John 8:44, made these statements about him. Jesus told his listeners that the devil has NO truth in him. He told them lying is the devil's native tongue. He told them the devil is a liar at his root and core. He is the father, or originator, of lies. In saying these things about the devil, Jesus exposed the devil for who he really was and is, particularly in contrast to whom Jesus was demonstrating Himself to be. Jesus wanted His listeners to trust Him and believe in Him; Jesus came from the Father and only spoke what the Father gave to Him to say and teach to them – all of which was completely and thoroughly true.

In addition to this, when Jesus told His disciples He would be going away to the Father but then sending the Holy Spirit to them, He called the Holy Spirit the Spirit of truth. As the Spirit of truth, He would guide them into all truth. This also meant He would steer them clear of all lies, deceit, and attempts by the devil to mislead them from following Jesus and the truth. His voice would ring with the same truth as the Father and the Son. He would be with us always, ready and available to lead, guide, and keep us in the truth.

In my own life as I've walked with God, I can affirm and attest to the fact God is a God of truth in every way. I've never experienced a time where God has ever contradicted

Himself in anything He said to me – whether through His Word or by His Spirit. Additionally, I have seen God work and move in my life in ways consistent with who He says He is. He has been faithful to come through when I have needed Him most and has always kept His promises to me. In my darkest hours and lowest points, He has been true to His Word to never leave or forsake me. He has been and continues to be a tried-and-true friend, and for that I am extremely grateful. His voice in my life has been the voice of truth.

To sum up, God is who He says He is. He does what He says He will do. When God makes a promise, He keeps it. He does not lie. We can trust Him with our lives and our destinies, both in this life and beyond this life. Because His voice always resonates with the truth, we can recognize His voice by this distinctive – because He cannot and will not ever LIE to us.

The Third Distinctive of God's Voice: *God's Voice Is The Voice of Encouragement*

Along with truth, encouragement is part of God's native language. God wants us to believe we can be who He has called us to be. He wants us to believe we can do what He has called us to do. He wants us to know with Him, nothing is impossible. So, when He speaks to us, we should be able to recognize His voice because His voice will resonate with encouragement.

In contrast to this, the voice of our enemy will bring discouragement. Our enemy will tell us the opposite of what God tells us. Instead of telling us we can, the voice of the enemy will tell us we can't and will list any and all reasons why we can't be or do what God says we can be or do. The end game in this, of course, is to keep us from trying or, if we try and fail, to get us to quit altogether.

God knows as we follow Him, the road will be rough. There will be successes and failures, victories and defeats. We will advance and move forward, and we will have our setbacks at times too. God knows all this, and His voice still comes to encourage us, move us forward, and onward in Him. It's not the falling God is concerned about; it's the getting back up to keep going that is His concern for us. He is leading us to a destination point – and the ultimate victory will be getting there, finishing the course, and completing the journey. The promised land of eternity with Him awaits us, and He will provide every help and resource we need daily, including the strength and resolve that comes from His encouraging voice.

One of the supreme examples in the Scriptures of God's encouragement is the account of the Israelites' journey into the Promised Land. Before they were about to enter the Promised Land, they sent 12 spies – one representative from each of their tribes – to survey and check things out in the land and then come and report back to all the people their findings. In Numbers 13:26-33, they had just returned from surveying the land and were reporting what they saw to the people. Ten of the spies brought back a mixed report; the land was indeed good, they said, but the people living in the land were bigger and stronger than them. In their own eyes, these ten spies viewed themselves as too small and not powerful enough to overcome the people of the land and take over the land.

Two of the spies – Joshua and Caleb – disagreed with the other ten spies. They were convinced they should go and take possession of the land and they could do it. They could overcome and defeat the current residents of the land. In Joshua chapter 14, these two men attempted to bring the people's focus back to God by reminding them if God was pleased with them that He would surely lead them into the land and give it to them, just as He promised He would do. They encouraged their brethren not to be afraid of the people living in the land. They reminded them the LORD was with them and the protection of the people of the land was gone. As a result, they believed victory awaited them and the land would soon be theirs.

If the people of Israel just took a moment and recalled their recent history and how God had just delivered them out of Egypt AND defeated Pharoah and his mighty army, this alone would have refocused them and helped them to see what lay before them was just another enemy God could and would help them defeat in bringing them to live in their new home.

Sadly, in that moment, no one but Joshua and Caleb seemed to recall all of this, and so fear and discouragement set in and won the day. The people grumbled and complained against God and accused Him of wrongdoing – of leading them out of Egypt only to have them either die in the wilderness or at the hands of the people of the land to which they were now heading.

God, for His part, was not pleased with His people and this response and decision they made in those moments. Initially, God threatened to wipe them all out, but Moses spoke up and told God not to do it or else all the nations would hear about it and say God, who brought His people out of Egypt, was not able to finish the job and bring them into their own land. Moses asked God to forgive the people for this sin.

God did just this – He did forgive them. But He also punished those who would not believe both the good report of Joshua and Caleb nor believe God, who had already done such great things for them, would continue to do great things and lead them successfully into the Promised Land. The punishment was twofold: the ten spies, who brought a negative report and spoke discouraging words to the people, were struck down dead by a plague from the Lord. God silenced the voices of discouragement once and for all time.

The other part of the punishment was anyone over the age of 20 would not see the Promised Land but would die in the desert. The very fate they had feared would now become their fate due to disobedience and unbelief. In spite of God's encouragement from all He had done for them up until that point and the encouragement from Joshua and Caleb, the people refused to be propelled by this encouragement to believe God for greater things still and continue on their way with the assurance God, who was with them, would continue to be there and fight for them.

Fast forward now forty years later, and all of those whom God said would die in the desert have died. All of those who were not older than twenty are now forty years older, and Joshua and Caleb are still alive, well, and ready to enter the Promised Land. Moses died at Mount Nebo, and Joshua took over the leadership of the people of Israel. God announced to them it was time to enter the Promised Land and take hold of it. The very first words He spoke to Joshua before they went up for the first time were words of ENCOURAGEMENT.

We find these words in the opening of the book of Joshua. God reiterated His promise to give them the land they were heading into and to give them victory over the people there. God encouraged them to be strong and courageous and to obey His words as revealed to Moses. God promised once again to be with them wherever they went, which was to be the foundation of their strength and courage for what lay ahead of them. They believed Him wholeheartedly and entered and took the land as promised. Toward the end of the book of Joshua, these words are found:

"So the LORD gave Israel all the land He had sworn to give their forefathers, and they took possession of it and settled there. The LORD gave them rest on every side, just as He had sworn to their forefathers. Not one of their enemies withstood them; the LORD handed all their enemies over to them. Not ONE of ALL the LORD's good promises to the house of Israel failed; EVERY ONE WAS FULFILLED" (Joshua 21:43-45).

The older generation out of Egypt refused to believe God and heed His voice of encouragement. As a result, they were punished and died in the desert. They did not see the promised land, lay hold of it, and live in it. Their children were given the same opportunity as they were and heard the same voice of encouragement from God, but unlike their predecessors, they believed God and acted in obedience to His voice.

As a result, everything God promised them came to pass. He helped them and gave them victory and enabled them to take hold of and occupy the Promised Land as their new homeland. He then gave them rest on every side. As a result of this, they have given us a picture of what God's voice is and what He wants His voice to be for us: a voice of encouragement, not discouragement.

A voice that inspires faith, hope, and obedience – which creates an opportunity for Him to act on our behalf and bring about the promises He has made and He fulfills for those who will heed His voice and take Him at His word.

In the New Testament, there are also examples of God bringing encouragement to His people. His voice of encouragement is consistent throughout Scripture. For instance, in Luke 22:31-32, Jesus told Peter and the other disciples Satan had asked permission to sift them like wheat. Jesus reassured them He had prayed for them that their faith would not fail. He also told Peter when He turned back around he was to go and strengthen his brothers.

Basically, Jesus was saying they were going to be tried and they were going to fail. But He had prayed for them so their failure was only a temporary setback and not a permanent one. In telling them this, Jesus was encouraging all of them. "I know what's about to happen – you are all going to be tested and all will fail me, but know I've prayed for you. Your failure will only be a temporary setback in your faith. You will turn back and be strong again." Jesus saw the end – them turning back – and He encouraged them. They were heading into a difficult time, but they would come out of it okay in the end.

In the letter to the Hebrews, the writer told his readers to run the race before them with perseverance and keep their eyes on Jesus, the author and perfecter of their faith. The writer mentioned a great cloud of witnesses – those who had preceded them in their own journeys of faith – to point out to his audience there are those who have gone before them and finished their journeys too. These same ones who had gone before them also faced challenges and difficulties but overcame them through their continued faith in God.

So now they must do the same, drawing strength from the stories of those who had gone before them and ultimately from Jesus himself, their great high priest, and the one who was the beginning and the end of their faith and hope.

These examples and witnesses of Scripture show us clearly God's voice can be recognized as one that brings encouragement to us. God knows we need it daily and constantly. Life is not easy, and the challenges we face in our own walk of faith can feel overwhelming and insurmountable at times. All the while, God longs to be right there in our ears reminding us we can make it with His help. He encourages us to keep on going and not to give up.

Even for me in writing this book, God encourages me every morning to get up and keep writing. He helps me formulate the thoughts and ideas that go into this work, and He keeps me focused on the goal and the daily steps needed to achieve the goal. His encouraging voice is life over death, victory over defeat, and the push that creates the momentum we need to keep moving forward in the right direction.

The Fourth Distinctive of God's Voice: *God's Voice Inspires Faith and Hope*

When God speaks to us, He wants it to have an effect on us. One of the primary things He is hoping to achieve is to get us to place our faith in Him and follow Him. Faith is believing what we cannot see, but more than that, faith leads to action. Faith is about following God into the unknown and seeing where He leads us. Fortunately for us, many have gone before us and did just that, and their stories of faith and action and the outcome of their faith and action have been recorded for us. In reading the accounts of their faith, we can draw courage and confidence to do as they did – to hear God speak to us, to believe, and to follow Him ourselves.

The Scriptures contain these stories and accounts of people who heard God speak to them, acted on what they heard, and saw God bring about the things He told them. In the letter to the Hebrews, the writer lists several of the main characters whose faith in God serve as examples for us to learn from and imitate. In chapter 11, the writer lists Abel, Enoch, Noah, Abraham, Isaac, Jacob, Joseph, Moses, Rahab, and a host of others who put their faith in God and saw what God did in response to it. His voice to them inspired faith in them, and in acting in faith as a response to His voice, they witnessed God move in their lives and on their behalf.

Probably one of the best examples of God's voice inspiring faith is when Jesus called His disciples, and they left their lives behind to follow Him. Perhaps at the beginning, they thought they would check things out, and if something seemed off, they could just fall back to their previous professions and lives. As time went on, and they heard His words and saw the things He did, their initial decision to follow Him became a permanent one.

Through revelation, they saw He was more than a good man, a teacher, or a prophet. He was the Son of God. In hearing His voice, they were hearing God the Father's voice. Their initial curiosity gave way to a life commitment. They believed and trusted Him with their lives. He inspired faith and commitment in them, and so He was able to make them into apostles and entrust them with continuing His work after He went to be with the Father.

The Scriptures declare an important truth about faith. Paul, in his letter to the Romans, says "Faith comes from hearing the message" (Romans 10:17). In this context, Paul is talking about the gospel. However, the principle is true beyond just the gospel. Everything God speaks to us is meant to inspire faith in us. The opposite is also true – if something we hear does not lead us to a response of faith or trust in God, then it is safe to conclude it is not from God and not His voice.

It's as simple as that. God never intended hearing His voice to be complicated. He never meant it to be for experts only or to require a degree of some kind to be competent enough to hear from Him. Faith is important to Him and something He longs for each of us to have when we hear Him. He knows faith will lead us to the right response and action. So, He fills His words with the seeds of faith and all we have to do for those seeds to take root and bear fruit in our lives is hear and agree with them, letting them sink in and take hold in our hearts.

Along with faith, God intends His words to inspire hope in us. Hope is similar to faith, but hope is about an outcome in the near or distant future. Hope is the confident expectation God will bring about good in our lives, regardless of how things look at the present time. So, when God speaks to us in the midst of trial or tragedy, His words and His voice will be recognizable by the hope they inspire.

The prophet Jeremiah is a great example of God's words inspiring hope in the midst of tragedy, suffering, and pain. In Lamentations 3, Jeremiah was feeling the effects of the Lord's punishment of His people. They had suffered defeat at the hands of their enemies. Many of the people had been killed. Their towns and cities had been destroyed. They had been taken from their homes to Babylon where they were living as exiles.

In this situation, Jeremiah found hope. He knew because the Lord loved His people, none of this spelled the end for them. God had promised He would once again visit them with His goodness, compassion, and mercy. They would one day return to their land, rebuild the ruins, and live there again. They were still His people, and He was still their God. He would always show His faithful love to them, and in this, Jeremiah put his hope in God.

It didn't matter how things looked at the present time or how awful they had been. Jeremiah tethered himself to the expectation God would renew, restore, and refresh His people at the time He had already determined to do so. It was not a matter of if but when. When the time came, God would be true to His word of restoration, and in this, Jeremiah found hope.

God has made us many great and precious promises too. The greatest of them all is Jesus is going to return for us someday. When He does, He will take us from death to resurrection life once and for all. We will never die again. We will live with Him and enjoy His presence forevermore.

In the in-between time, we have this life. It has its ups and downs, as we all know. One solid and consistent thing in this is God's voice, which speaks to us unshakeable, unwavering hope. He is with us, He is working for our good, and He will bring about the ultimate good in the end for us. To recognize His voice is to hear His words of hope to each of us, and to draw strength, inspiration, and joyful confidence from them.

The Fifth Distinctive of God's Voice: *God Will Correct Us, Not Condemn Us, When We Sin*

The Scriptures make it clear ALL have sinned and fall short of the glory of God, which is sinless perfection. None of us is perfect, and in this life, we will never be perfect. Even in Christ, we have times when we stumble and fall – where we fail, fall short, and miss the mark. When we do, God will speak to us even then. It may come as a surprise to some, but His words will come to correct us, not to condemn us.

When I learned this in my relationship with God many years ago, it set me free from the fear of making mistakes and of punishment associated with my failures. I would sin or fail in some way and dread what might be coming my way as a consequence for what I had done.

It was in this context God came and helped me to see things from His perspective, which was radically different from my own. God was not looking to punish me for my sins – He already punished sin on my behalf by having Jesus die for my sins and take the penalty for sin I deserved. So, in God's mind, the punishment for sin was a done deal.

God was looking rather to help me see my mistakes and learn from them. What was wrong with what I did? Why did I do it? How can I do it differently next time? In posing these questions, God made my sins a teachable moment where He could help me see where I went wrong and then show me the right way to do it going forward. Then, knowing the right way, His Spirit would empower me to do it the right way the next time. God's end goal was to correct me and correct my course, not to condemn me and heap punishment, guilt, or shame on me.

This is a radical departure from what many of us have come to know and believe about God. For some reason, we have this notion that God's anger can flare up in a moment, and when it does, watch out! You don't want to be on the receiving end of His anger. The reality is, God has revealed Himself as SLOW to anger and PATIENT with us. Because He is slow to anger and patient, He's not just waiting for the next slip-up of ours to pounce on us and dole out punishment. We are His dearly loved children in Christ, and

He is our loving, kind, and affectionate Father. Because He is our Father and we are His children, He will discipline us, but in love – not in anger or exasperation. He takes a long view of things and sees the end in mind He wants to achieve in us. He does not get discouraged or lose heart when our progress is slow or when we have a bad moment, day, or week. He knows we are weak and fragile. He longs to help us, set us going the right way, and provide everything we need so we can "go and sin no more."

The Scriptures are in full support of these ideas. John writes in his gospel Jesus was not sent into the world to condemn the world but to save it (John 3:17). Paul, in his letter to the Romans states, "There is now no condemnation for those who are in Christ Jesus." (Romans 8:1) John further states in one of his letters when we confess our sins now to God, He will be faithful and just to forgive us and cleanse us of all unrighteousness (see I John 1:9). Taken together, God longs to save us from our sins, forgive us, and cleanse us – not condemn us.

When we do sin as believers, and we certainly do, God longs to discipline us in love as a Father disciplines His children. He does so in a way that trains us to be godly and holy just like He is. His discipline leads to righteousness and peace. He does this for our good, for it is His highest aim in our lives to bring about all that is good in us and for us (for these ideas, refer to Hebrews 12:1-13). As Paul stated in Ephesians – we are His workmanship, meaning our lives should reflect and reveal His handiwork to form and fashion us as He pleases. Paul also stated with confidence in his letter to the Philippians "He who began a good work in you will carry it on to completion until the day of Christ Jesus" (Philippians 1:6).

God has priorities. His priority is not punishment. His priority is perfecting us, completing what He started in us. We will never be "perfect" in this life, meaning we will still have times when we fail, stumble, and fall. In those times, we will have a loving, gracious Father there with a hand extended to help us back up again and get us going on the way once more. He is more concerned with progress than perfection, with perseverance and a "try again" mentality than with how many times we fail. Knowing this, we can be assured when He speaks to us about our failures; we don't have to be afraid of what He might say. He is for us and not against us, and He is all-in when it comes to seeing us succeed and finish the race set before us.

Let's look at two examples of these principles in action from the ministry of Jesus. In one instance recorded in John 4, He met a Samaritan woman at a well in a Samaritan town and asked her to draw some water for Him. Their conversation quickly turned to Jesus offering her a drink that would cause her to thirst no more. When she showed an interest in having what He was offering, He asked her to go get her husband and come back. It's at this point she confessed she did not have a husband, and Jesus then added she had had five husbands and the man she was with was not her husband.

When Jesus spoke these words, she recognized He must be a prophet to know these things about her. She tried to change the subject, but He was able to direct it back to His ultimate purpose. He revealed to her He was the long-awaited Messiah, and so His offer of living water now became an invitation to know Him and satisfy her heart's thirst in Him.

As a result of this encounter, the woman became a believer in Jesus and told her whole town about Him. They in turn came out to see and meet Him for themselves and also became believers through their own personal encounters with Him. Jesus spoke to her error in trying to find satisfaction for her soul outside of Him, and in doing so, He corrected the course of her life by directing her to the one true source of living water. Instead of condemning her for the life she had lived, He redirected her so from that point on, her life would be lived for Him and in Him.

The other example from Jesus' life I want to look at is found in John chapter 8, where the teachers of the law and Pharisees brought before Jesus a woman accused of being caught in adultery. They pointed out to Jesus that according to the law, the penalty for what she had been caught doing was stoning to death. They wanted to see if He would agree with them or not. At first, He didn't answer them but instead bent down and wrote on the ground with His finger. When pressed by them for an answer, He stood up and said they could stone her but only if none of them had ever sinned themselves.

At this, one by one they all dropped their stones and left. They all knew there was no one without sin but God, so none of them met the criteria Jesus gave them for stoning her. Left alone with the woman, Jesus then turned to her and asked her where her accusers were and if there was anyone left to condemn her. He didn't imply she hadn't done what she was accused of; He merely asked her if there was anyone left who condemned her for what she had done. She acknowledged to Him all of her accusers were gone. Then He told her He was not going to condemn her either. Instead, He told her to go and leave her life of sin.

"Go now and leave your life of sin" (John 8:11). These words of Jesus are the summation of what God says to us when we sin. He is not out to condemn us but to save us, forgive us, correct us, and send us off on a different course

– His course for us. His voice can be recognized as the one that will point us away from sin and lead us to Him to receive forgiveness, mercy, grace, and the power to leave our sin behind and follow in His more excellent ways. Hearing correction and discipline isn't always easy; but as He is motivated by our good because of His love for us, He can be trusted to speak the right things to us when we need them and to lead us always into His right ways.

The Sixth Distinctive of God's Voice: *God's Voice Will Speak Wisdom to Us*

King Solomon, who was perhaps the wisest person to ever live, stated "The fear of the Lord is the beginning of wisdom" (Proverbs 9:10). This means wisdom starts with God – knowing Him, respecting and revering Him, and recognizing Him as wisdom's source and foremost expert. King Solomon knew this from experience. At the beginning of his kingship, the Lord came to him and told him to ask for anything he wished. Solomon, recognizing how large a responsibility it was going to be to be king of Israel, asked God for the wisdom to rule well.

God honored him for this and honored his request by giving him wisdom that surpassed all the wisdom of the people of the world at that time. His wisdom became so well-known even royalty from other nations traveled to Israel to meet Solomon and listen to his wisdom. God turned Solomon's simple request into something that would bless both him and his people as well as the leaders and people of the nations they governed.

Wisdom, simply put, is the knowledge of the right, best, and most excellent course of action to guide our day-to-day choices and decisions. Godly wisdom enables you and me to know and do God's will as we go about our daily lives. One of the roles Jesus said the Holy Spirit would have in the lives of believers would be to teach us all things and guide us into all truth. That means we as followers of Jesus have the source of all wisdom living inside of us, ready to guide us and lead us as we seek Him and His direction for our steps.

Paul in his letter to the Colossians told them in Christ are hidden all the treasures of wisdom and knowledge (Colossians 2:2-3). So, when we come to Christ and give our lives over to Him, these treasures of wisdom become ours to have and access when and as we need them. We don't have to look outside of Him to find what we need to live this life right and well. It is all to be found in Christ alone.

James in his epistle told his audience "If anyone lacks wisdom, he should ask God, who gives generously to all without finding fault, and it will be given to him" (James 1:5). God encourages us to seek Him out for the wisdom we need when we are unsure or undecided about an issue and what course of action we should take in the middle of it. His voice will be recognized as the voice of wisdom and good counsel to help us and assist when we need it most.

As an illustration of this, let me share a personal example. When I was a freshman in college, I was involved in a minor car accident in which another person hit my car from behind as I was preparing to pull out of a parking lot. The guy who did it, was about my age, and seemed apologetic for having hit my car. We exchanged information, and I told him I would get back to him to let him know what the repair costs would be and get his complete car insurance information so the incident could be properly reported and taken care of by the insurance company.

A few days later, I called him, and his attitude had changed. He was annoyed and gave an indication he didn't want to own up or take responsibility for what he had done. After our conversation, I was upset and felt like the guy was not going to do the right thing unless I notified the police or took another type of legal action against him to get him to pay for the damage he had done.

Before I did anything though, I took the matter to prayer. I asked God for wisdom about what I should do. What the guy had done was wrong and to try and evade responsibility for it was even worse. As I prayed, I began to sense from God I was to forgive the guy and drop pursuing the matter with him any further. It was a difficult decision to make, but in the end, it's what I chose to do.

I ended up only fixing the broken taillight on my car – as that was something by law I had to fix and have in good working use. The dent in the bumper I just left alone and never fixed or replaced it. The repairs, while they didn't cost me a fortune, still were a lot of money for me as a college student with limited extra funds – since most of my funds at that time were going towards paying for college.

Over time, my feelings over being wronged would fade away. I stood by my decision to forgive the person who damaged my car and wouldn't pay for the repairs. I never saw or heard from the guy again, and my car was just fine minus the dented bumper. I truly believe God's wisdom guided me the right way in this situation, and I am thankful I sought Him out for the direction I needed in dealing with this matter.

Whether it's a large or small matter, it all matters to God when it comes to us. He loves us so and delights to hear from us whenever we call on Him. He knows life will bring us difficult situations and decisions, and it does not bother

Him at all when we seek Him for answers in the midst of them. He is the source of all wisdom, and He longs to share it with us and give us what we need and lead us on the right paths. His voice can be recognized as the voice of wisdom, shedding light where we need it so we can see and act with clarity and certainty in all of life's choices and decisions.

The Seventh Distinctive of God's Voice: *When God Speaks to Us Through Others, He Will Not Contradict Himself*

I know this distinctive sounds similar to the first distinctive we began with, but it is also slightly different. That's why I felt the need to include it here. God speaks to us directly, as He did with Moses and many others throughout history. God will also speak to us through angels and our fellow believers. Unfortunately, since our enemy the devil likes to masquerade as one representing the light, we need to be sure we are not caught off guard by someone claiming to speak for God but whose message goes against the truth already revealed to us.

Many a false belief or even worse, a false religion, has been built on the premise God was speaking or revealing Himself to a person through an angel or directly to that person and then to others. The sad fact is that their words or messages were not tested properly or held up to the standard of the Scriptures for comparison and scrutiny. Had that been done, perhaps many errant messages and messengers would have been exposed and their messages and ideas rejected.

Paul's instructions to the Thessalonians are fitting concerning this: "Do not treat prophecies with contempt but test them all; hold on to what is good, reject every kind of evil." (I Thessalonians 5:20-22). This is not only sound advice and instruction, but it will also keep us from falling into error in what we hear and listen to as well as train us to be proactive listeners who take what we hear and put it to the test to determine if it's worth holding onto or merely discarding.

In the early church, there were many teachings going around that were off the mark, and one of the main jobs the apostles had – as evidenced by their letters – was to expose these teachings for what they were and safeguard the churches from being misled and deceived by false teachers and false teachings. So, what these apostles did was twofold: they reminded their readers of the truth they already knew, and they pointed out how to recognize a false prophet or teacher when one came into their midst.

As to the teachings of false teachers and prophets in New Testament times, there appeared to be a number of them the apostles had to counteract. One of these was Gentiles had to be circumcised and keep the Law in order to be accepted by God. Paul specifically addressed this school of thought in his letter to the Galatians. In the letter, he showed the Galatians the promises of God were obtained by faith, not by following the law.

Paul used Abraham as the supreme example of this. Abraham lived before Moses and thus before the law was given. Abraham received a promise from God he and his descendants would be blessed by God and a blessing to all the nations of the earth. Abraham, at that time, did not have any descendants because he and Sarah did not have any children. Yet Abraham believed God for what he did not yet have. At the appointed time by God, Isaac was born to Abraham and Sarah.

Through his faith in God, he received what had been promised by God. Through faith, Paul pointed out, they all received the grace of God that brought salvation, eternal life, and membership in the family of faith that traced its roots back to Abraham. In laying all this out for them, Paul reminded them of the truth they were taught and had accepted. Since the teaching on circumcision did not agree with the teaching on grace through faith, it was to be rejected out of hand by them and dismissed and discarded as false.

The apostles also helped the new believers to recognize false prophets and teachers. Jesus made it clear in his teachings, trees (people) would be known by their fruit. The apostles tried to prepare the churches for the inevitable: false teachers would be among them, but they would be recognized by the fruit of their actions and lives. Among the fruit the apostles told the churches to look out for – besides their unbiblical teachings – were things like greed, fleshly and unholy living, and a greater focus on themselves than on Christ and Him crucified.

Peter also mentioned they despised authority and were bold and arrogant in their attitudes and words. They themselves were led astray and led others astray who listened to them and followed their teachings and example. However, they were headed for destruction and punishment. So, the apostles not only warned the churches to keep an eye out for them but also warned them to steer clear of them and not listen to their false teachings or follow in their unholy and ungodly ways. Many will claim to hear from God or have a message from him, but the true prophets and teachers will have lives consistent with their message and be an example worthy of following and imitating.

To sum up this distinctive, God gifts and calls people to be prophets and teachers. God also expects those He calls to live lives worthy of Him and only deliver messages He has given them through the Scriptures and the Spirit, who always speaks in agreement with the Scriptures. If a so-called prophet or teacher has fine-sounding words that go against what has already been revealed, their message is to be rejected.

Further, if their lives do not display a consistent pattern of godly and righteous living, then it is advisable to steer clear of them and not follow their example. God does speak through others, but He will not contradict Himself or alter what He has already revealed to us. If we will remember this as we earnestly seek to hear and recognize His voice in our lives, it will keep us from straying and falling into grave error.

The Eighth Distinctive of God's Voice: *God's Voice Will Draw Us Closer to Him*

Paul, in his letter to the Philippians, declared to them he considered all he once thought was valuable as garbage and as worthless compared to the surpassing greatness of knowing Christ Jesus (see Philippians 3:1-11). For all who believe in Him and claim to follow Him, this is the highest goal and greatest pursuit – to know Him. Even Jesus, as He prayed for His disciples and all those who would one day become disciples, stated He came to give them eternal life. Eternal life meant knowing the Father and knowing Jesus (John 17:2-3). It's correct to say through Jesus, God came close and near to us to draw us close and near to Him.

Nearness to God is a theme throughout the Scriptures. David is probably one of the supreme examples of someone who made his life about being near to God. His greatest desire, longing, and hunger was to be in God's presence, to dwell in God's house, to draw near to God, and to see God's face and be captivated by the beauty, glory, and majesty of the Lord. Such passion inspired him to write words such as these: "One thing I ask of the LORD, this is what I seek: that I may dwell in the house of the LORD all the days of my life, to gaze upon the beauty of the LORD and to seek Him in His temple" (Psalm 27:4). David's life was full of many things, but only one thing really consumed him like no other – and that was this desire to be close and near to God.

As I mentioned in another place, in Luke's gospel, he recounted a short but pointed story about Mary of Bethany, who also desired nearness to God more than anything else. In Luke 10, Jesus was visiting Bethany and was at Martha and Mary's home. Martha was preparing things for Jesus and her other guests (presumably a meal of some sort), and the expectation was that her sister, Mary, would be helping her with all of these preparations. Instead, Martha saw Mary sitting at the feet of Jesus and listening to Him speak. Martha pointed this out to Jesus and insisted Jesus tell Mary to come and help her.

Jesus' response in that moment made it clear to Martha and those present Mary had chosen the "better portion" and it would not be taken away from her. Martha was busy with many things, but Jesus told her only "one thing" is needed. Mary had chosen that one thing – to sit at Jesus' feet, to listen to Him, to give Him her full and undivided attention as He taught and spoke. Jesus applauded Mary's simple devotion in those moments and validated her decision to take and make time for Him.

A closer look at the things Jesus taught makes it clear Jesus warned His followers about things that would try to consume their thoughts, time, and lives. Whether food, drink, clothes, money, or other earth-bound things - Jesus, throughout His teachings, pointed His followers to Himself and to putting Him ahead of all other people and things. He summed this up with these words: "But seek first His (God the Father's) kingdom and His righteousness, and all these things will be given to you as well" (Matthew 6:33).

Jesus affirmed to His listeners the first and greatest commandment was to love the Lord your God with all your heart, all your soul, and all your mind. God comes first, and there is to be no close second in our lives. Nearness to Him is the number one priority on His heart as it concerns us and our relationship with Him.

Because God desires nearness with us, His voice and His words will be recognized by that ever-present and underlying theme. In all the years I've walked with God, I can attest this is true. God has made having a close, intimate relationship with Him priority number one in His dealings with me. His greatest desire, and the thing that has continued to pop up through every season and circumstance of my life, is for me to know Him.

Sometimes I get too caught up in other things – work, family, and the cares of this world, to name a few. I get busy, like Martha, with a great many things. When this happens, my relationship with God suffers neglect and does not occupy the highest place in my life. In those times, God will highlight where I have gotten off course and will draw me back to where He occupies the center point of my heart and life. He helps me to give those things their proper due while keeping Him first. Sometimes He will even call me to give things up entirely if they are pulling me away from Him. In everything He says, He is always leading me back to Him – never away from Him. By this I recognize His voice to me: always calling me close, drawing me near, and making Him the one thing I desire most of all in life.

We have one final question to explore about hearing God's voice. As we do, we will discover the keys that will launch us into the journey of a lifetime with Him.

CHAPTER TEN

How Should We Respond When God Speaks?

I love receiving wedding invitations.

Most of the wedding invitations I've received were from family members who were getting married. I love my family very much, and any chance to join them in celebration of a joyous occasion, I'm there. I don't think I could say no even if I wanted to. If I had something else planned for that day, I would change it, reschedule it, or cancel it. Without even thinking about it, my answer is, "Yes, I'm coming."

With every wedding invitation comes an RSVP card. This is how you tell them you're coming. You write your name on it and tell how many people you are bringing (so they can plan for enough food at the reception). They will usually include a self-addressed, stamped envelope so you can easily return your RSVP to them. Once you've filled it out and sent it, all that's left to do is go on the day. They know you will be coming and will be prepared for you because you have taken the time to respond.

There are other responses that could be given to the invitation too. Maybe I don't like this family member very much, so I just say, "No, I'm not coming." Maybe I have something else going on that day I cannot change or cancel, so my response might be I can't make it. Maybe I lose or misplace the invitation, get busy, and forget all about it. Afterward, when the day arrived, not only did I not attend but I didn't even remember the grand occasion in the first place. All of these could be other ways I respond to the wedding invitation too. My point is: when my family members sent me the invitation, they were looking for a response. They are hoping I say "Yes" and come, but there could be other possible ways I respond to their invitation as well.

In Matthew 22, Jesus told a parable about a king (God the Father) who prepared a wedding banquet for his son (Jesus). The time had come and everything was ready, so the king told his servants to go tell everyone who was invited to come now. But they refused to come! So, the king sent them out again to the streets and the street corners to invite anyone and everyone they encountered to come. Eventually, enough people said "Yes" to the invitation so the wedding hall became filled with guests.

In the same way, God has extended to us the greatest of all invitations. He has invited us to come and be in a covenant relationship with Him. We are not just the invited guests; we are the reason He is preparing a banquet in the first place! We are the guests of honor. Going even further, we are called to be the Bride of Christ Jesus, who is the Bridegroom. The wedding banquet is for us, and He is looking for a response from us to this grand invitation. The first and greatest response we can give to Him is our "Yes." Yes, I will come. Yes, I will be in a covenant relationship with you. Yes, I will be the bride to your bridegroom.

Once we enter into this covenant relationship with Him and give Him our "Yes," He has more He wants to say to us. Being in a relationship with Him, He wants to speak to us regularly and often. When He does, He will be looking for us to answer and respond to Him. The responses we give are like keys that unlock doors in our lives that let Him come in and fellowship with us. Many adventures in Him await our response to Him when He speaks.

Moses would have never seen God's amazing signs, wonders, and deliverance of the Israelites out of Egypt had he chosen to ignore God when God came and spoke to him. When God speaks, He is giving us an opportunity to know Him more, to discover what He is like, and to experience Him in a greater way. Our responses are therefore crucial to what happens next, so let's look at what those responses should be if we want to open up the doors God puts in front of us and see what happens next when we do.

When God Speaks, Pay Attention and Listen

I know it seems like the most obvious thing to say: when God speaks, the first thing we should do is stop, pay attention, and listen. However, each of us can relate to the fact that sometimes when we are talking to someone, they are not paying attention or listening to what we are saying. Sometimes too, we are the ones not truly listening when someone is speaking to us. When this happens, it can potentially send the message to the speaker we don't value them or what they have to say. This is not the kind of message we would want to give to a close friend or family member. How much more then, when God speaks, we do not want to give off the message to Him we're not listening and don't consider Him or what He has to say to us as important.

God's words are a treasure to us. They are life to us. They literally can be the difference between life and death for us. So, it is crucial when He does speak for us to make every effort to listen to Him and pay attention to what He has to say. Had Noah not listened to God, none of us would be here today. He and his family are the only survivors of the massive, global flood. Had they chosen not to listen to God and pay attention to Him when He told them to build the ark and get ready for the flood that was coming, they, too, would have perished when the flood came. The key to their survival was listening and paying attention to God's voice when He spoke to them.

All throughout Scripture, God tells people to hear His voice, listen to Him, and heed what He is saying. Conversely, God chastises His people for not listening to Him and ignoring what He has to say. One of Jesus' patented phrases to His listeners was, "He who has ears, let him hear" (Matthew 11:15; 13:9 and 43; Mark 4:23; Luke 14:35). Given this phrase is recorded in 3 of the gospels, I suspect it was something Jesus said regularly to his listeners.

He is reminding and commanding them to truly listen and pay attention to what He has to say. He even compares those who listen and don't listen to His words to those who built their houses (their lives) on either sand or rock. Those who build their lives on listening to and paying attention to His voice and doing what He says are like those who build a house upon a foundation of rock. When the storms come and beat against that house, the house withstands it because its foundation is strong and sure. Our lives, therefore, depend on us listening to God's voice, heeding His words, and making them the foundation for our lives.

So where should we begin? Our first response to God's voice should be to listen and pay attention. It is the starting point of the response God is looking for from us. We need to be like Samuel who said to the LORD, "Speak, for your servant is listening" (I Samuel 3:10). Samuel uttered these words the first time He heard God speak to Him, and from that point on, Samuel built his life around hearing and listening to God's voice. We should do the same. Hear what He has to say to you and I. Listen and make every effort to pay attention. This is the starting point, and everything else that comes next depends on us making this first step in response to God's voice.

When God Speaks, Remember What He Says

God also wants us to remember what He says to us. Everything He says is valuable and important, so we do well to remember what He says. In Psalms 105:5, David penned these words: "Remember the wonders He has done, His miracles, and the judgments He pronounced..." Jesus, in sharing His last meal with His disciples before His arrest and crucifixion, told them when they took the bread or the cup, the symbols of His body and His blood, they were to do so in remembrance of Him. Jesus also said of the Holy Spirit, "He would remind you of everything I have said to you" (John 14:26). So clearly, remembering what He has done for us and said to us is important to Him.

In the Old Testament, one way the people remembered the things God had done for them was to set up memorial stones as a reminder of the miracle or wonder God had performed on their behalf. For example, in Joshua chapter 4, when the people of Israel cross the Jordan River and enter the Promised Land, they are instructed to take 12 stones out of the middle of the Jordan River, one for each tribe of Israel. They set these stones up at Gilgal to serve as a memorial of them crossing the Jordan River on dry ground. This was also supposed to remind them they had crossed the Red Sea on dry ground. These mighty acts of the Lord their God served two purposes: "That all peoples of the earth might know that the hand of the LORD is powerful and so that you might always fear the LORD your God" (Joshua 4:24). When their children saw these stones and asked about them, they were to tell the stories of what happened and what the stones meant so the knowledge of God and what He had done for them would be remembered by those who experienced it and then passed on to the next generation so they too would remember and know the LORD.

There are a number of ways we can remember what God says to us. One thing we can do is write it down. Keeping a journal of the things God speaks is a great way to remember them and to go back and remind ourselves of what He said to us. Another way to remember, which seems to be a lost and dying art, is to memorize what He said. Scripture memorization in particular can be very helpful in recalling to our mind what God has spoken to us. The Scriptures also encourage us to meditate on God's word (see Psalms 1).

Meditation on God's word means to think it over, to ruminate on the words He's spoken, to repeat it to yourself, and even to talk about it and process what it means. As we take the time to do this, His words become more solidified in our hearts, minds, and memories. Finally, we do well to remember the Holy Spirit is with us and can help us remember and recall the things God has spoken to us.

So, what are some of the things God wants us to remember? He wants us to remember He is with us always

(Matthew 28:20). He wants us to remember He loves us always (Jeremiah 31:3). He also wants us to remember His promises, His answers to prayer, and the victories He has won for us. He wants us to remember who we are to Him. He wants us to remember who He is and not forget Him. It's interesting to note that as Jesus partook of the Last Supper with His disciples, He instructed them to do it in remembrance of Him. Remembrance is important to God and vital for us if we want to properly respond to God and all that He speaks to us.

The longer you and I walk with God, the more personal history we build up with Him. This personal history we build up with Him has immense worth and value. As we look back over our lives and God's dealings with us, we can see His hand, and His presence in our lives. We can see the consistency of His character. We can see His divine plan working out. We can see how He ordered our steps and our life's circumstances.

All of this taken together becomes and forms our testimony, our story of who God has been and who He is for us. This testimony is powerful and useful. It can be wielded as a weapon against the enemy of our souls (Revelations 12:11). It is also the story of the gospel fleshed out in human form and example, which serves to show those around us who God is and encourage and persuade them to know Him even as we have known and know Him. Remembering is key in all of this, so we do well to make remembering what God has said to us and done for us one of our responses to Him when He speaks to us.

When God Speaks, Have Faith and Trust Him

One of the most fundamental responses to hearing God's voice is faith. God wants us both to believe what He said and trust the One who said it. Time and time again, both throughout the Scriptures and in history, God has shown Himself to be a keeper of His word. God is not a man, that He should lie (Numbers 23:19). When He says He's going to do something, He follows through and does it. He keeps His promises and shows Himself true and faithful. He has a name and a reputation to uphold, and He takes that very seriously. So, it is only fitting and natural He wants us to have faith in Him and trust Him and His words.

When we respond to God with faith and trust, it pleases Him. He also rewards all of those who put their faith and trust in Him. The writer of Hebrews said this very same thing: "And without faith, it is impossible to please God, because anyone who comes to Him must believe He exists and He rewards those who earnestly seek Him" (Hebrews 11:6).

On the flip side, He promises that those who put their trust in Him will never be put to shame (Isaiah 28:16, and also Romans 10:11 and I Peter 2:6). He will not let us down or make us look bad for trusting Him because if He did, that would reflect poorly on Him as well. It would show the world He is not trustworthy and we were foolish to put our trust in Him. Knowing all this, we can have confidence our faith and trust in Him will be rewarded and vindicated. All of those watching us to see if God will come through or not will get to witness God move and work on our behalf because we trust in Him.

From beginning to end, the Scriptures record the stories of people who heard God's voice, who believed what He said was true, and who trusted Him to do things He told them He would do. Noah built an ark before God sent the massive flood to destroy all life on earth, and he and his family trusted God to keep them safe in that ark during all the time the earth was flooded until it was safe again to get out and resume life on earth. Abraham trusted God to grant him a son in his old age, and so Isaac was born to him and Sarah as God had promised.

Moses trusted God to perform all the signs and wonders He told him He would do in delivering the people out of slavery in Egypt. Moses and the people of Israel witnessed God work these great wonders in Egypt and ultimately part the Red Sea and lead them safely through on dry ground. Then God returned the waters to their place and drowned Pharaoh and his army, who had been pursuing them.

Gideon trusted God to give him victory over the Midianites with a mere 300 men. Elijah believed that God would indeed not send rain on the earth except at his word, and it did not rain for 3 years in Israel. Shadrach, Meshach, and Abednego believed God could deliver them from being harmed or killed in Nebuchadnezzar's fiery furnace. He was with them and protected them in there. Not a hair on their heads was singed nor did their clothes burn up or smell like smoke.

Mary trusted God to enable her to conceive as a virgin, and nine months later, Jesus was born into the world. All of these examples show people who trusted God and saw God do what only He could do. They heard God speak, and their response to Him was faith and trust.

In my own life, I can testify of time after time when God has told me to trust Him, and when I have done so, He has been able to come through for me in ways only He can. I remember a time when I lived in San Francisco during the years I was a pastor and was helping to plant a church there. I was supporting myself by working for a hotel in downtown Union Square. We had reached a slow period, and my full-time hours got cut down to a couple of days a week.

I was leading worship the Sunday morning that same week, and one of the songs I had selected had the words "Jesus is going to make everything all right." I really felt the Holy Spirit emphasizing those words to me as we sang them, so I stopped and shared what was going on with work and how my hours had been drastically cut. In spite of this, I was filled with faith at that moment and declared to the congregation that somehow Jesus was going to make my situation all right, even though at that time I didn't know how he would do it.

Over the course of the next two weeks, the manager of the hotel I was working at found some slow period odd jobs he had me do since it was slow and it was a good time to do those things around the hotel. He found enough work to get me through that first week. Then, a friend of mine who worked for the same hotel chain mentioned other hotels within the chain might have some shifts available. She encouraged me to check with two in particular who might be able to have me fill in a few days. It turned out I was able to get 3 shifts out of this. All told, I was able to get enough hours that week for full-time work as well.

After this two-week period, things picked up again at my hotel and my schedule returned to full-time. I was able to share again with the congregation my testimony from the previous two weeks and how God had come through and made things "all right." I did not suffer any loss of income during that stretch, but most importantly, I put my faith and trust in God to make a way for me, and He did so. He had promised to make things all right, and as I trusted Him and took Him at His word, He did just that.

So, faith and trust are essential responses God is looking for from us when He speaks. We benefit because He blesses and rewards our faith and trust in Him. He gets the praise, worship, and glory for being who He is and doing what He does for us.

When God Speaks, Do What He Says

The response to God of faith and trust has a complementary partner: obedience. In trust, we believe and watch God do what He says He is going to do. In obedience, God watches us do what He says He wants us to do. These two things are two sides of the same coin – two equally important halves that comprise one complete whole.

God wants us to put His words into action and practice. James, in his epistle, makes these two important statements concerning action in response to God's words: "Do not merely listen to the word and so deceive yourselves. Do what it says" (James 1:22) and "As the body without the spirit is dead, so faith without deeds is dead" (James 2:26).

This last statement comes as the summary to James' brief discourse on how faith and action work together and how action completes faith. It's not enough to say we believe God's word; we must also put faith into action. Obedience to God's word, then, is that action and response God desires from us when He speaks.

Jesus also made this same thing very clear in His teachings. In His parable about the wise and foolish builders, He equates the wise builder to the one who hears His words and puts them into practice. The only safe and sure foundation for our lives, according to Jesus, is to hear His words and obey them. Just look at Jesus' commission to His disciples prior to His ascension into heaven. He told them to go and make disciples of all the nations and to teach them to obey everything He had commanded them.

The disciples, first and foremost, were to obey Jesus themselves. Their ministry's focus was also to teach others to do the same things they were also doing. Obedience was to be the response to their message and their teaching, even as obedience was the response Jesus was looking for to His message and His teaching.

It's also interesting to note the ministry goal of apostles, prophets, evangelists, pastors, and teachers is to equip the saints for "works of service" (Ephesians 4:11-12). Earlier in this same letter, Paul stated "We are God's workmanship, created in Christ Jesus to do good works, which God prepared in advance for us to do" (Ephesians 2:10).

From this we see that God has works for us to do. He is not merely calling for us to hear Him, receive from Him, and let Him do for us. He has things planned for us to do too. Our response when He calls or commands us ought to be obedience and action.

His words are also meant to train us to do right and good (2 Timothy 3:16). Training involves repeated action and doing. God fully intends for us to act on His words and not merely listen or hear them. The book of Acts is called just that because it is a record of the acts of the apostles. The apostles did not just sit around and do nothing! They heard from God regularly and did what He told them to do. In the same way, when God speaks to us, He is looking for us to act repeatedly and regularly.

Obedience to God has two aspects – doing what the Scriptures say and doing what the Holy Spirit tells us. First of all, we are to obey His words as contained in the Scriptures. His Word contains His guidance and instruction to us for righteous and holy living as well as for loving Him and loving others. The Scriptures contain things we should make a habit and discipline of putting into practice. He reveals to us His will in His Word, so we know what He wants done. In this regard, then, the Scriptures are an invaluable source for knowing and obeying God's words.

The Holy Spirit, who lives in believers, also should be listened to and obeyed. The Scriptures lay things out generally that the Holy Spirit shows us where, when, and how to fulfill specifically. For instance, we are commanded to go and make disciples of all nations per the Scriptures. As we listen to and follow the Holy Spirit, He can and does guide us specifically to the people and places He wants us to go to fulfill this command.

In my own life, this has meant going to San Francisco, Colombia, England, Kyrgyzstan, and South Asia – as well as to my neighbors, family, friends, and coworkers nearby. The Spirit helps us and enables us to know how to fulfill the commands and instructions we find in the Scriptures. I have covered this at length already in this book, but it's important to state it again: hearing God's voice involves the Scriptures and the Holy Spirit, and obedience to His voice also involves both. It's not one or the other – it's both, just as God intended it to be.

Our obedient responses will also have positive results and outcomes. God has set up obedience to Him to result in blessings for us and others. Jesus is the ultimate example of this. His obedience to come to earth, to humble Himself, and to go to the cross on our behalf has resulted in blessing to the entire world, and to all of humanity. Paul stated it this way: "For just as through the disobedience of the one man the many were made sinners, so also through the OBEDIENCE of the ONE MAN (JESUS) the many will be made righteous" (Romans 5:19, emphasis mine). Christ's obedience has yielded and resulted in the maximum possible blessing to all of mankind.

Everyone who believes and comes to Him can be justified, made righteous before God, saved, and granted eternal life through Him. While our obedience will never accomplish what Christ's obedience accomplished, the principle is still true concerning obedience. Our obedient response to God's words will result in blessing to us and others.

Not only this, but our obedience pleases God and shows Him we love Him. Obedience pleases Him because it brings Him praise, worship, and glory. He delights to receive our praise and worship, so when we obey Him, He accepts it from us as a beautiful and fragrant offering and expression of our gratitude and love for Him in response to His great love for us (see Paul's words in Romans 12:1). The Scriptures also declare love for God involves obeying His commands and doing what He says (I John 5:3). Love for God is expressed in action, specifically towards our neighbors, and our brothers and sisters in Christ (I John 3:16-18 and I John 4:19-21). Love is God's greatest command to us, so when we act in love, we are obediently doing what He has commanded us to do.

So, in view of all this, it is vital we make obedient actions one of our primary responses to God when He speaks to us. We need to make sure we act on what we hear from Him and couple our faith in Him together with obedient action. In this way, our response to Him speaking to us will be full, complete, perfect, and pleasing in every way.

When God Speaks, Agree With Him

Agreeing with God is a powerful thing. When we come into agreement with Him, He can release things in and through our lives that further His kingdom and accomplish His will here on earth. So, one of the responses He is looking for when He speaks to us is agreement with Him and what He has said.

Consider the example of Mary, the mother of Jesus. What was her final response to what the angel Gabriel had told her? "I am the Lord's servant...May it be to me as you have said" (Luke 1:38). With these words and in this moment, Mary agreed with God concerning her role in God's plan to bring Jesus into the world. She agreed to conceive, carry Jesus to term, give birth to Him, and be His earthly mother. God's plan at that moment hinged on Mary's agreement, and she expressed her willingness to be used by God in this way. No wonder she found favor with God; her heart was turned towards Him, as evidenced by her agreement with Him concerning her role in His plans.

Think about the example of Jesus Himself. He agreed to come to earth. He agreed to do the Father's will while He was on earth. He agreed to give His life for our sins and be our ransom and our redemption. In the garden of Gethsemane, before His arrest and the events that would lead to His crucifixion, we get a glimpse into His heart and into His agreement with the Father. Here are Jesus' words in the moments before His arrest: "My Father, if it is possible, may this cup be taken from me. Yet not as I will, but as you will" (Matthew 26:39). When He prays again, He utters these words: "My Father, if it is not possible for this cup to be taken away unless I drink it, may Your will be done" (Matthew 26:42).

These words give us insight into Jesus' commitment to the Father and to the Father's will. Jesus lived His life on earth doing what He saw His Father doing and saying what His Father gave Him to say. His life was one of complete surrender and submission to the Father's will. Then, here at the end, at the culmination of everything, He stayed true to His commitment to agree with the Father concerning the Father's will and the purpose for which He had come to earth. His death would be excruciatingly painful in every way, but He was committed to seeing it through. In fact, He made it clear to His disciples at another time He freely and willingly was going to lay down His life.

In John 10, He told them this: "The reason my Father loves me is that I lay down my life – only to take it up again. No one takes it from me, but I lay it down of my own accord. I have the authority to lay it down and the authority to take it up again. This command I received from my Father" (John 10:17-18). He had already decided what He was going to do. He had given His accord – His agreement – to the Father's plan.

He would lay down His life for us, but He would also be raised to life again. He would then be exalted and seated at the right hand of the Father. He would become the Savior of all who would believe in Him. To all of this, Jesus said "YES," and we are all the beneficiaries of His agreement with His Father's will.

So how do we make agreement with God our response to Him when He speaks to us? We can do this in a number of different ways. For one, we can agree with Him concerning the promises He has made to us. In 2 Corinthians 1:20, Paul makes this statement: "For no matter how many promises God has made, they are 'Yes' in Christ. So, through Him, the 'Amen' is spoken by us to the glory of God."

The word, "AMEN," literally means "so be it." It is a word that indicates agreement with what has been said, in this case, agreement with all the "Yes" promises of God in Christ. We, therefore, can agree that all of God's promises are true and they are "Yes" for us and will be fulfilled for us.

Another way we can make agreement with God our response to Him when He speaks to us is in our prayers. Jesus taught His disciples to pray, and we are familiar with what is called, "The Lord's Prayer." In that model prayer, Jesus makes this declaration: "Your kingdom come, your will be done on earth as it is in heaven" (Matthew 6:10). These words are an expression of our agreement with God that we want to see His kingdom come and His will done on earth – just as it is in heaven. So, we can agree with Him by knowing what His kingdom is like and knowing what His will is and praying for those things to be so here on earth – in our lives and in the lives of those around us and among all the nations of the earth. What He wants for us, He wants for everyone.

The Father promised Jesus all nations as His inheritance, so when we pray in agreement with God's kingdom come and His will to be done on earth, we are praying in essence Jesus would receive His inheritance of people from every tribe, nation, and tongue. We agree with God they would belong to Him and gladly welcome His rule, His reign, and His will in their lives. So, praying as Jesus instructed us to pray is a means of responding in agreement to what He has spoken to us.

We can do this in prayer another way. In I John 5:14-15, John says if we ask God for anything according to His will, He hears us. Not only does He hear us, but we can have confidence that we will have what we asked of Him. The key words here are "According to His will." When we pray in agreement with His will, we can be assured He will hear and answer those prayers. So, by knowing His will and turning our prayers into requests of agreement with His will, we are aligning ourselves in agreement with Him once again.

Last of all, we can do as Mary and Jesus did. We can agree with God in faith and action. We can believe, as Mary did, that the things God said about us are true and accept His will for our lives by giving Him our agreement with His will. Like Jesus, we can live out our lives each day in agreement with His will for us. We can do as He shows us to do and act as He shows us to act. We can choose to follow Him daily and make the most of every opportunity He gives us to walk in agreement and alignment with Him. We can be who He says we are and so agree with Him about what He says about us. A life of agreement with God and what He says to and about us is a powerful way to respond to God when He speaks to us.

When God Speaks, Humbly Submit to Him

James and Peter, in their letters, state the following: "The Lord opposes the proud but gives grace to the humble" (James 4:6 and I Peter 5:5). James follows this up by saying, "Submit yourselves, then, to God. Resist the devil, and he will flee from you" (James 4:7). Taken together, the Lord is looking for those who will respond to Him with humble submission when He speaks to them. The fact is, those who are proud, stubborn, and unwilling – the Scriptures declare these ones are in opposition to God and He to them. I don't know about you, but I do not want to be in opposition to God. If and when we do so, we are giving place to the evil one in our lives, whether unknowingly or not.

So, this makes the decision we face quite simple: if we choose humble submission to God, it pleases Him, and He will give grace to those who do so. If we choose pride and are unwilling, we are giving a place in our lives to the evil one, but more than that, God will oppose us, and we will be opposing Him and His will for us.

As always, Jesus is our great example of one who walked in humble submission. Paul states in Philippians we should imitate Christ's attitude in this way. Jesus was and is God. He is equal in nature to the Father. Though this is all true of Him, Jesus CHOSE to become nothing, to become a servant, and to humble Himself and take the lowest place among mankind. His attitude of humble submission enabled Him to be obedient and give over His life to death on the cross! (see Paul's words in Philippians 2:5-8).

This was not the end of the story for Jesus. He was raised to life again, and God exalted Him to the highest place and gave Him the name above every other name. It is to the name of Jesus that every knee will bow, and every tongue will confess – in heaven and on earth and under the earth – that Jesus Christ is Lord (see Philippians 2:9-11). Jesus' humble submission to God's plan to save mankind through His death resulted in good coming to us and Him being glorified, exalted, and seated in the highest place above all in the universe.

Though what awaits us is not the exact same thing that awaited Jesus, we still have wonderful things ahead for us too. We are promised we will be with God forever. He will give a crown of life to all of those who persevere in faith and endure to the end. One key for us to do this is humble submission. Our hearts being turned towards God and bowed to Him is key to being able to fully receive all He has promised and prepared for us in eternity.

In this promise, though, there is also a warning. The warning is simply this: do not harden your hearts. The most dangerous thing to you and me in this life is a hardened heart towards God. The writer of Hebrews reminded His readers of the dangers of this very thing. An entire generation of Israelites died in the wilderness and did not enter the Promised Land because their hearts were hardened in unbelief towards God. They refused to believe He would truly give them the promised land, and so they refused to enter it. They believed the report of the 10 spies who had surveyed the land and found it was good, but who concluded the people there were too big and too strong for them. For them, it was not worth the risk or the effort to go in and try to take the land.

In response to this, God told them they would not enter the land and they would die in the wilderness. Israel had to remain in the wilderness until all of that older generation had died off. They missed their chance to enjoy the bounty and goodness of their own homeland because their hearts were not right before God. Had they chosen humble submission to God, they could have entered and taken the land He had promised to them. Their unbelief and their hardness of heart serve both as an example and a warning to us not to miss out on all God has for us by making the same fatal mistake they made.

Though all of this is true, we should not be discouraged by it. The fact is, we can humbly submit ourselves in response to God and His words to us. When we do this, God gives grace to the humble. When we choose humble submission to God, we give God the opportunity to pour into our lives all the grace we need for whatever situation we are in and whatever circumstances we are facing. What looks impossible is made possible by His grace. His grace comes in response to our humble submission and enables us to move forward in spite of opposition from anything that tries to get in our way or stop us. His grace is always greater, so all we have to do to receive it and step into it is humble ourselves before Him.

We must admit we can't do this on our own and we need Him. He is pleased and honored by this, when we confess we need Him and look to Him for help. He will supply grace, and we will be empowered to finish the course set before us. Humble submission is the response that opens the door to Him and His grace in our lives, so we do well when we choose this heart attitude as our response to Him.

When God Speaks, Be Joyful

God's words to us should bring joy to our hearts. After all, the heart of God towards us is He loves us. He loves us so much He sent His Son for us. The gospel message is good news to all of mankind. The angel who appeared to the shepherds to tell them of Jesus' birth declared, "Do not be afraid. I bring you good news of great joy that will be for all the people. Today in the town of David a Savior has been born to you; He is Christ (the Messiah) the Lord" (Luke 2:10-11). Indeed, the news of Jesus' birth and coming brought great joy to all who heard it, for they had been waiting for and looking for God's promised one. So, when it was announced He had finally come, it brought a response of great joy from those who heard it.

When we consider God's plans for us or His promises to us, they should fill us with great joy and delight. God is good! He is a good Father. He is a good provider. He has good things in store for us, His children. The mere mention of those things should make us glad and fill us with gladness. Believers who know God and know His words should be the most joyful of people. God is for us and not against us. He, for all time, has made a way for us to know Him and be with Him forever. He is with us now and always. In a world full of bad news, darkness, and gloom, God's words to us should be a bright, shining beacon of hope, joy, and gladness.

In Psalm 119, believed to be a Psalm of David, David extols God's words and expresses His delight in them. Consider the following excerpts: "I rejoice in following your statutes as one rejoices in great riches" (verse 14); "Let your compassion come to me that I may live, for your law is my delight" (verse 77); "Your statutes are my heritage forever; they are the joy of my heart" (verse 111); "I rejoice in your promise like one who finds great spoil" (verse 162). David valued God's words greatly. He valued knowing and following them. To David, God's words were a source of comfort, joy, and delight. In this, David shows us a proper and fitting heart response to God and His words.

When I stop and consider for a moment God could have chosen not to speak to us or reveal Himself to us, I am all the more delighted He did speak to us and make Himself known to us. He could have stayed silent and left us all to die. When we became cut off from Him by our sin, He could have left us out in the cold. Fortunately for us, this is not what He did! He has made Himself known to us. He gave His Son for us. He has both told us He loves us and showed it in a clear and unmistakable way. All the more, then, we should be delighted and joyful God has spoken and still speaks to us. Joy and delight in His words, then, are a most fitting and proper response to Him when He speaks to us.

When God Speaks, Worship Him

In Romans 12:1, Paul states since God has shown us mercy, our only fitting response to this is to offer our bodies as living sacrifices, holy and pleasing to Him, which is our reasonable act of worship. He gave His Son for us; we, therefore, offer our lives to Him in response and in return for all He has done for us. This is the true heart of worship – offering our lives to Him to live for Him in response to all He has said and done.

In Revelations, we get a glimpse into heaven – what's going on there and what it is like. One thing that characterizes heaven is worship (see Revelations 4:8-11, 5:9-14, 7:9-12, 11:15-19, 15:1-4, and 19:1-10). Recorded in the book of Revelations are several instances where angels, redeemed saints, and others are worshipping God and the Lamb (Jesus) for the things they are doing or the things they have done. They are praising God for who He was, is, and eternally will be. Worship is their fitting response to all of this. How much more, then, should it be on earth as it is in heaven! Our response to God – to who He is, to things He has done, is doing, and will do – should also be worship.

The Scriptures also show people giving thanks and praise to God for all He has done and for the greatness of who He is. These things are also aspects of worship since they are a fitting and pleasing response to God for everything He is to us.

In Psalm 95, the psalmist incorporates all 3 of these elements – thanksgiving, praise, and worship – into the psalm and invites others to come and join in. In verse 2, the psalmist declares, "Let us come before Him with thanksgiving and praise Him with music and song." In verse 6 and 7, the psalmist goes on to say, "Come, let us bow down in worship, let us kneel before the LORD our Maker; for He is our God, and we are the people of His pasture, the flock under His care." So, thanksgiving, praise, and worship are essential in our response to Him.

I personally try daily to express thanksgiving, praise, and worship to God. As He does things throughout the day that are clearly His hand at work, I try to take notice, stop, and say, "Thank you." When He reveals an aspect of His nature, I try to stop and marvel at the wonder of who He is. Sometimes I will recollect His past works in addition to the real-time things I see Him doing. Also, I try to view every aspect of my day – whether at work, at home, on the road, with people, or all alone – as opportunities to live life as an act of worship unto God.

It's not just when we have ministry opportunities or are at a church gathering we can or should express our worship to God, but worship should be a lifestyle and seen in everything we are and do. The Scriptures declare we should do all unto the glory of God. With this in mind, worship should be our daily and habitual response to God for all He says and does for us.

When God Speaks, Love Him Back

I John 4:19 says, "We love because He first loved us." God initiated love with us. It was while we were still sinners and God's enemies Christ came and died for us (see Romans 5:8 and 10). We were not looking for God. It was Jesus who came to seek and save the lost. Had God continued to wait for us to turn to Him, it's likely He would have been waiting for all eternity for us to do so. Instead, at the right appointed time, He sent Jesus to seek us out and find us and to become the means of our salvation and reconciliation through the cross and His life given for us. God started all of this, not us.

We are always acting in response to Him and the things He has said and done. The response God longs for the most, in view of His mercy and love for us, is for us to love Him back. He wants a love relationship with us. He yearns and longs for us to be close and near to Him. He desires to pour out in abundance His love into our lives and to bring us to experience the heights, the depths, the lengths, and the breadths of His love for us – now and for all eternity. However, this is not automatic; it takes us turning to Him and responding to Him, putting ourselves in a relationship and position to experience and encounter Him and His great love for us.

King David understood and grasped this. In reading through the Psalms David wrote, we can see David's jubilant expressions of love for God for loving him, of desire to be close to God, of longing for God's presence, and of adoration for God's person. David loved all the great things God had done for Him and all the wonderful gifts God had given to Him. David's greatest love and desire was for God Himself above all.

Consider the following example from the Psalms: "God, You are my God. Earnestly I seek you; I thirst for you, my whole being longs for you, in a dry and parched land where there is no water" (Psalm 63:1). Further in this same psalm, David declares, "Because Your love is better than life, my lips will glorify you. I will praise you as long as I live, and in Your name, I will lift up my hands. I will be fully satisfied as with the richest of foods; with singing lips, my mouth will praise you" (Psalm 63:3-5).

Over and over again, David lauds the Lord's love for Him and responds with praise, worship, and an intense desire and longing to be in God's presence all the days of his life and beyond. For David, God was the most valuable thing and the greatest prize worth having in life. In response to God's great love for him, then, David made it His aim to worship, honor, and love the Lord with all of his heart.

In the New Testament, Paul echoes these same sentiments expressed by David. Paul, in his letter to the Philippians, stated the things in life he valued and treasured the most prior to coming to Christ he now considered rubbish, worthless in comparison to the surpassing greatness of knowing Christ Jesus. For Paul, Christ was now the prize he wanted the most, and he spent the rest of his days on Earth pursuing Christ with all of his heart.   Paul   knew who he was before Christ saved him and showed him mercy. He knew the unworthy and undeserving things he had done, and yet he also knew God had shown him mercy, forgave him, and displayed unlimited kindness, patience, and love to him.

In response to this, Paul worked hard to fulfill the commission and calling he had received from God. He endured suffering and hardship gladly if it meant knowing Christ Jesus and making Him known to others. His life was one He lived as a response to God's love for Him and displayed for all his great love for God in return.

Similar to worship, love as a response to God should be something we walk out daily and something we turn into a lifestyle. It should permeate everything we are and everything we say and do. Every situation we find ourselves in can be an opportunity to express our love for God as a response to His love for us. We can show Him our love by trusting Him fully, by obeying Him, by loving others, and so on. God will provide us endless opportunities to express to Him our love for Him. Loving Him is not only the first and greatest commandment, but it also should be our greatest happiness and joy in life.

The Holy Spirit, who lives in us, will guide and direct us to these opportunities for expressing our love for God. We simply have to remain sensitive to Him and follow Him as He leads us. As we do, God's love can move full circle – His love for us will be in us and expressed through us back to Him and to others. His love will become a never-ending flow between Him and us – touching both heaven and earth. So, let us eagerly choose love as our response to God when He speaks and interacts with us.

When God Speaks, Take It Personally

The last thing I want to say about a proper response to hearing God's voice is He wants us to take personally the things He says. For example, John 3:16 says, "God so loved the world that He gave His one and only Son, that whoever believes in Him shall not perish but have eternal life." YOU and I are the "whoever" He is talking about here. We have to put our names, ourselves in that place. God loved ME. He sent His one and only Son for ME. If I believe in Him, I will not perish but will have eternal life. God's dealings with us and His love for us are, in their very essence, individual and personal. This is everyone without exception. That's YOU and ME.

A tragic mistake I have sometimes made and I have seen others make is to think God will do certain things for others but not for us. I remember praying for one guy years ago to be healed of back pain. He had injured his back on the job. My teammate and I prayed for him and then checked in with him to see if he noticed any decrease in the pain. He said the pain still felt about the same. Then he went on to say he believed in healing and what God can do, but he was convinced it was for others and doubtful it was for him.

In that moment, we asked him to confess his unbelief to God and give it over to Him. We asked him to see and believe that God, in this moment, wanted to heal HIM. He sincerely prayed all of this, and then we prayed for him again. Guess what? His back pain was healed in that moment! The moment he decided God's love and healing power was FOR HIM, the moment he decided to make God's words personal, was the moment He opened the door for God to come in and bring healing into his own life.

We must take what God says and make it personal. We must apply it to our lives. God does speak specifically to us individually. Each one of us is responsible for pursuing knowing God and finding out the specifics He has that relate to our own lives. Yes, there are things God speaks to all of us generally and universally. Even those things require, at the most fundamental level, an individual response.

When we consider Jesus' time on earth, He ministered to the masses and large crowds. A lot of times, He took time for individuals. The tax collector Zacchaeus was one of those individuals. In Luke 19, Jesus was on His way to Jericho. Zacchaeus wanted to see Jesus, but he was short in stature. So, he ran on ahead of the crowd and climbed a tree to get a better view and give himself a chance to see Jesus when He passed by.

The amazing thing is when Jesus reached the spot where Zacchaeus was perched in the tree, Jesus saw HIM! Then He said these words to Zacchaeus: "Zacchaeus, come down immediately. I must stay at YOUR HOUSE today" (Luke 19:5). Jesus paid Zacchaeus a personal visit that day. Zacchaeus was one Jesus had come to seek out and to save.

For a few moments, Jesus left behind the ninety-nine for the one. In this moment, Zacchaeus was the "one" Jesus had come to find. He was sent into the world to save the world, for sure; but in this moment, it was ALL about saving this particular son of Abraham.

In my own life, I have endeavored to take all God says personally, especially the things He speaks to me as part of our personal, ongoing relationship. In listening and responding to His voice, I have discovered who I am to Him, and I have learned the specifics of His plan and will for my own life. Listening and responding to His voice personally has led me all over the world. It is what led me to write this book. It is what led me to use and develop the gifts He has given to me. It has led me to different friendship connections and partnership alignments.

Most of all, it has changed me, because I'm not who I was before encountering Him. His goodness and love are things I have taken very personally. As I have done this, He has been able to pour into my life His mercy, grace, and faithful love in abundance. I am not the same and will never be the same. My whole life is built around hearing His voice, taking what He says personally, and responding to Him in the ways He is looking for me to respond.

My RSVP to His glorious invitation was and is and will continue to be a resounding, "YES!" Yes to knowing and walking with Him. Yes to what He wants. Yes to where He's leading. Yes to walking through the doors He opens. Yes to the journey and the adventures along the way. Yes to the final destination, where I will see Him face to face and be with Him forever!

This moment is a NOW moment. If you have read this book in its entirety, thank you! I hope it has blessed and benefited you. But reading it from cover to cover is not enough. NOW is the time to act. Everything I was inspired to write here is for YOU and applies to YOU. In this moment, you have to take all He has said and done personally. Own it for yourself and apply it to yourself. Respond to His initiative to take the time and make the effort for you. He wants you to know Him - so say "Yes" to Him and His invitation and say it NOW.

This is His invitation to you and for you: walk with Him and talk with Him. Speak to Him and listen to Him. Learn to hear His voice and follow Him. Take what He says personally. He came for you. His Son died for you. He wants you to be reconciled to Him. He wants you to be a son or a daughter. He wants you to join Him in the journey He has already planned for your life. Saying "Yes" as your response to Him for it is the starting point to the most extraordinary life you could ever have or know in this earthly life. Begin today if you haven't begun already. Take what's been given here and put it to use. At the end of your life, you will not regret having heard God's voice and having responded – now and every day for the rest of your life.

FINAL THOUGHTS

"My dove in the clefts of the rock, in the hiding places on the mountainside, show me your face, let me hear your voice; for your voice is sweet, and your face is lovely" (Song of Songs 2:14).

This statement of longing from one lover to another captures the heart of God for you and me. He wants us to long for him this way because that's also the way that He longs for us. He desires a closeness and a nearness to us and wants us to feel and desire that towards Him.

The key to starting to hear His voice and to hearing it throughout our lifetimes is a simple desire to know Him, be close to Him, and walk in an intimate relationship with Him. "Show me your face. Let me hear your voice."

Jesus made this possible for us by coming to earth and being the sacrifice for our sins. The veil was torn, and access was purchased and granted into the Holy of Holies – the secret place of God's glorious and awesome presence. And while He is indeed Holy, Majestic, Great, and Awesome – He is also love – infinite, perfect, everlasting love. He has been calling all throughout human history and will continue to do so until the end for those who will accept His invitation to know Him personally. It's bought and paid for – we simply have to say "Yes" to Him and take Him up on His invitation.

In doing this over the course of my life, I have had my ups and my downs, my hot and my cold times. God has remained true and constant through all of that, and He has helped me to stay true and constant in my pursuit of knowing Him. Life is indeed a marathon and not a sprint. The call of God to us is to an everlasting covenant with Him. It is lived out steadily – one step at a time, one day at a time. I never judge my relationship with Him based on how I'm doing or how I'm feeling on any given day. Feelings change and they come and go. My pursuit of Him and my relationship with Him is greater than all of that. It is the highest goal of my life and the end goal towards which the days of my life are heading.

When viewed this way, I can enter each and every day with the right frame of mind. I was made for Him. I was created to know Him. I was equipped by Him to hear His voice and follow Him. He has demonstrated loud and clear He wants a relationship with me. He has spoken this to me by His words and His actions. Though I stumble and fall, He and His desire for this remain unchanged. I can pick up and start again, safe and secure in the knowledge He wants me. I am His and He is mine.

So go for it with all you've got! Make time for Him and make room for Him. Listen for and learn to hear His voice. Become familiar with it so when He speaks, you know it's Him and you give Him the time and space to say to you what He wants to say. Then respond accordingly in whatever manner is appropriate to what He's saying and what He's looking for in those moments. You will never regret it, but not only that, when you and I receive that rich welcome from Him into eternity with Him, full and overflowing joy will be ours in His presence forever. To that end, I live and breathe, and I hope you will too. God bless you as walk with Him, hear His voice, and never leave His side.